W9-ATY-652

Tell It Together

Tell It Together

Foolproof Scripts for Story Theatre

Barbara McBride-Smith

August House Publishers, Inc.
LITTLE ROCK

With thanks to my librarian buddies,
LaVonne Sanborn and Jonette Ellis,
who started me on this adventure.

—B. M-S

Published 2001 by August House Publishers, Inc.,
P.O. Box 3223, Little Rock, Arkansas, 72203, 501-372-5450.

See the first page of each fiction script for adaptation permissions.

*The scripts in this book are designed for use in classroom
and educational settings. Public performance of the scripts is
limited to free-admission productions in educational settings.*

Printed in the United States of America
10 9 8 7 6 5 4 3 2 1   HC
10 9 8 7 6 5 4 3 2 1   PB

LIBRARY OF CONGRESS CATALOGING-IN-PUBLICATION DATA
McBride-Smith, Barbara, 1944–
Tell it together : foolproof scripts for story theatre / Barbara McBride-Smith.
p. cm.
Includes bibliographical references.
ISBN 0-87483-655-7 (hardcover) — ISBN 0-87483-650-6 (pbk.)
1. Children's plays, American. 2. Readers' theater. I. Title.
PS3563.C33367 T4 2001
812'.54—dc21   2001003737

Executive editor: Liz Parkhurst
Editor: Joy Freeman
Cover photograph: Shannon Drawe
Cover and book design: Joy Freeman

The paper used in this publication meets the minimum requirements
of the American National Standard for Information Sciences—
Permanence of Paper for Printed Library Materials, ANSI Z39.48-1984.

AUGUST HOUSE, INC.   PUBLISHERS   LITTLE ROCK

Contents

Introduction

A Note from Barbara McBride-Smith

I have been writing this book for twenty-something years. Well, sort of. As a teacher, a librarian, and a professional storyteller, I have been developing and field-testing these scripts with real kids in real classrooms and in hands-on workshops for more than twenty years. I have shared my ideas and scripts with colleagues in my own school and in schools across the U.S. In turn, teachers, students, and storytellers have used my materials and given me incredibly helpful suggestions for making them better. The result is: these story scripts work! As I sit here alone at my PC writing these introductory words, I feel as though hundreds of teachers and students are crammed into this room with me saying: "We've done it together!"

The hardest part of compiling this material into a book has been writing the introduction. That's because I never read introductions myself. I'm a busy person, always eager to get on to the *important* stuff in a book. Nevertheless, I shall press on with my introductory remarks because I hold dear certain truths that explain how I work as an educator and a storyteller. These truths are basic and full of common sense.

Here they are:

1. **Everybody is a storyteller.** It's absolutely true. Oh, I agree we become storytellers in different ways. Some of us are born storytellers. Some of us, through hard work, achieve the title "Storyteller." And some of us, through no conscious effort of our own, have storytelling thrust upon us. I was lucky enough to have been born into storytelling. But many of the best educators I know are thrustees. Storytelling has become a means of survival for them in a postmodern world where children and adolescents are more attuned to oral and visual media than to information via print. However we get there, we are and should be storytellers. Telling stories is integral to what makes us human beings.

2. **The people who know most about teaching are those folks who do it every day in real classrooms with real kids.** The world loses track of this fact

because educators are too busy in the trenches and too short on time to write about their art. It has taken me more than twenty years to start putting my successes on paper. I'm sure I've forgotten a significant percentage of the best stuff I've done, but this book is an attempt to document and share a small portion of it. Long before I became a known commodity as a professional storyteller, I was a good teacher and a good librarian. (I still am.) When I create or find something that works with kids, I recognize it! And like good educators and storytellers everywhere, I want to pass it on. I do so with thanks and credit to all the teachers, librarians, and students who have helped me create these scripts and who continue to change them to suit their own needs.

3. **Learning to tell stories should be active, energizing, open-ended, and painless for the learner and the teacher.** The only absolute rule you must live by to be a storyteller is: *have fun!* Storytelling is a serious art form that must not be taken too seriously. Allow your students room for creativity. They want to change the words? Let them! They want to write a new ending? Let them! Allow the stories to empower them. These scripts are only the beginning. They will lay a foundation. Students will *experience* the stories, not just hear them. They will get their mouths and minds around the words, take the words off the page, and make the story work orally. They will realize that in storytelling, less is more. Most importantly, they will be communicating, not just saying words.

4. **It's the process that's important here, not the product.** You and your students may very well produce a theatrical piece that is so fantastic it must be put on a stage and taken on tour. The P.T.A. could invite you to perform it for parents. At the very least, you'll probably want to show it off to another group of kids. But letter-perfect productions is not what this book is all about. I'm the first to admit that many of my Story Theatres have been experiments. In allowing kids to be in control of the process, I have experienced creativity gone overboard. But what they have learned about communicating through story, and what I have learned about them as kids in charge of their own learning, I wouldn't trade for all the Tony Awards in the world.

There, I've done it! I've written an introduction. Whether you read it or not, I'm glad to have it off my chest.

Questions and Answers about Story Theatre

What is Story Theatre?

Story Theatre is Readers Theatre on steroids. That's how I begin my workshops. The description gets a laugh, but it's accurate. Story Theatre begins with the best techniques and discipline of Readers Theatre, and then breaks all the rules. It grows and expands into something unpredictable. The movement from page to stage is initiated by the students, whether you the teacher are ready for it or not. The younger they are, the sooner it will happen. They'll ask: "Can we get rid of these scripts and say the story in our own words?" If you are brave enough to say "Yes!," you have just crossed the line between Readers Theatre and Story Theatre. Now you must be willing for the creativity of your students to run amuck. Let them add gestures, sound effects, music, costumes, props. Just keep reminding them: We are about the business of *telling a story;* does this add to the telling or detract from it? They will learn the art of negotiating as well as the art of storytelling.

So, what is Story Theatre? It is a storytelling vehicle that allows a group of people to tell a story together. It is an opportunity for involvement, interpretation, and interaction with the story and with other learners.

What are the most important values of Story Theatre?

- **Beginning storytellers can learn the art of performing in a supportive, non-threatening environment.** Many people, young and old, have a fear of public speaking. Most can overcome it, or at least learn to compensate for it. Story Theatre gives them the chance to work through their shyness and fears, build their self-confidence, develop their performance skills, and quite possibly become solo storytellers. But even if a participant never gathers the courage to tell a story without a supporting cast, that individual has had a grand experience performing as part of an ensemble.

- **Non-readers and non-verbal students can help tell the story.** Special education students in my school are eager and willing to provide sound effects, music, and mime in our storytelling productions. Kindergartners can learn, repeat, and re-create dialogue faster than any age group I've worked with. Even four-year-olds can become a speaking chorus.

- **Story Theatre supports a whole language philosophy of learning.** It combines the skills of all the language arts—speaking, listening, reading, and writing. In assuming responsibility for how they will most effectively communicate a story, students become authentic users of language.

- **Story Theatre is a participatory sport.** Performance drives this storytelling vehicle. Everyone has a strength, and the combined strengths of the group are what make the show go on. The only one who eventually has to sit on the sidelines is the teacher/director. Whew!

- **Story Theatre is inexpensive and easy.** Scripts are not hard to come by. You'll find enough in this book to last you several weeks. More importantly, these scripts will serve as models and impetus for students to seek out stories and write their own scripts. You won't need elaborate sets or costumes. A mere suggestion of costume (king wears a crown) or a hint of location (cardboard tombstone) fills the bill just fine. Your students, particularly if they are adolescents, probably know current music better than you do. Let them find places in the story to use it. They'll be delighted to bring you their favorite CDs. Imagination is free. Making it manifest "on stage"—which, by the way, can be simply a classroom or a library—becomes the doing of the learners.

- **Story Theatre is fun.** And everybody knows that learning to tell stories should be fun. So, what are you waiting for?

What equipment do I need to do Story Theatre?

- **This book!** Just kidding. But it's a good place to start. You will need written scripts and binders to hold them. I prefer sturdy black ring binders. Whatever you use, be sure the pages turn easily, lie flat, and open easily for adding/removing pages. The cast members will progress—even without your permission—from reading the scripts word-for-word to using the scripts as props. Scripts can become guitars, umbrellas, serving trays, doors, crying babies—whatever the story demands. Left to their own initiative, they will soon substitute props for the scripts, put aside the scripts, and *tell* the story.

- **Stools.** These are essential. Buy them or borrow them. They turn an ordinary floor into a performance space. I use a combination of two heights—approximately 18" and 28"—arranged to accommodate each story. They must be sturdy enough to stand on. If they swivel, all the better, but that's a luxury more than a necessity. Each character in the story has a stool. Early read-throughs and rehearsals will take place with the actors sitting on their stools. As the cast learns the story and begins to deliver their lines without scripts, they may decide to add physical movement to their production. I recommend that you limit the movement to a small space. Remember, this is not conventional theatre with full blocking. It is text-oriented drama. Some of these plays are best done with most of the action taking place while the characters remain on their stools.

- **Music stands.** For most stories, I use two narrators. They are usually assigned the most lines in the story. While other cast members sit, turn, and move on or near their stools, the narrators remain stationary behind their music stands, which hold their scripts. They may sit on tall stools or stand on their feet. They may also be elevated on box platforms. Some casts may decide to keep the scripts in front of the narrators during performance—just in case someone needs a cue. Other casts may choose to remove the music stands and the scripts.

- **Wooden platforms.** These are not essential, but they do add variety and dimension to the staging of the story. Someone handy with power tools can construct these for you in an afternoon. I recommend beginning with one box, 12" high and 24" square. A goddess or a granny could be elevated on a stool atop this platform with other cast members arranged in front of them. A second box, 18" high and 36" square could hold two or three persons. Be sure that the platforms are sturdy but lightweight.

- **Costumes.** These are optional. The performers should be the first to suggest them. I recommend keeping them simple—no elaborate sewing or adherence to historical accuracy. Bedsheets make wonderful togas for Greek myths. Overalls can make a city slicker kid look like a farmer. Some of my casts have defined their characters by wearing hats. Others have made decorative signs to wear around their necks. Some troupes have decided to wear matching t-shirts.

- **Sound effect devices.** Children are especially creative when it comes to making noise. The younger your cast, the less you'll have to encourage them. I always have handy in my production area the following: a tape recorder, a Vibra Slap, whistles, a xylophone, tambourines, metal cooking pots with lids, kazoos, wooden blocks, sand paper, and wooden sticks. Once I demonstrate how a few of these might help in telling the story, my students take over and supply any other noise-producing devices they decide to use. I have made suggestions for sound effects in some of my scripts. Feel free to change, eliminate, or add more.

- **Props.** These need not be expensive or "authentic." They should enhance the interpretation of the story rather than distract the audience's attention from it. A magic wand made from a dowel rod and a cardboard star might be the perfect touch for a fairy godmother. A handful of fake money can make a miser appear more miserly. A picture of a minotaur will be far more manageable than the real thing.

- **Sets.** You won't need elaborate theatre sets for Story Theatre. Sparseness is the keyword. You need only a suggestion of a set. A couple of tall potted plants can be a forest. Stools arranged two-in-front-of-two simulate a car. A blue curtain with metallic stars pinned on it will create a celestial setting. A platform can be a house or a throne or Mount Olympus.

What makes this book different from other books about Readers Theatre, Chamber Theatre, and Story Theatre?

Every story in this book can be told by a group or by a single storyteller. Before I wrote them as scripts, I told them as stories. As a storytelling teacher, I introduce each script by telling the story. So, when the students begin to work with the script, they are dealing with something familiar. By the end of our production, every person in the cast knows his own lines, as well as everyone else's lines. Every cast member can tell the story solo. This is the most effective and efficient way I know to teach someone how to be a storyteller.

The stories in this book are kid-tested. I am a full-time elementary school librarian in Oklahoma. I work with students, ages four through twelve, every day. We create and re-create these scripts together, using literature that we discover in our library. When something in a program doesn't work, we change it or throw it out and start all over. We find new stories, do research for details, and download pictures from the Internet for our productions. We send out invitations via district e-mail. We involve parents in helping find simple props, costumes, and sets. We present our productions for other students in the school and ask them to write reviews of our shows. Not surprisingly, the "funny" stories always get the best reviews. So, you will find that many of the scripts in this book include kid-humor.

These scripts were not written for the purpose of being published in a book. They were written as *real* lesson plans and workshop activities for students and teachers who know what *really works*. When the opportunity came for me to put some of our stories in a book, I asked my students to help me choose the *best* ones.

And here they are!

MYTHS

King Midas

A Greek Myth

Scripted for Story Theatre by Barbara McBride-Smith

Cast of eight:

NARRATOR 1 (N1)	APOLLO
NARRATOR 2 (N2)	BARBER
MIDAS	SATYR
PAN	SOUND

N1: Long, long ago, there lived a king named Midas.

N2: King Midas was as foolish as he was greedy.

MIDAS: Oh, how I love gold! I wish I had all the gold in the world. I just can't get enough of it.

N1: One day, a music contest was held between two gods named Pan and Apollo.

N2: Pan was only a minor god, but he was a very popular music star. *(PAN clasps hands overhead, victory-style)*

ALL: *(clapping)* Yea, Pan!!!

N1: Apollo was a major Olympian god. In fact, he was called the god of music. *(APOLLO waves to the crowd—a stiff, royal gesture)*

ALL: *(clapping)* Yea, Apollo!!!

N2: Everyone knew that Apollo could beat anybody anytime in a competition of musical skills…

N1: But King Midas was the judge for the contest. And Pan was the king's best friend.

PAN: Hey, King! You and me—pals!
(PAN and MIDAS give thumbs up gesture)

N2: The big day arrived, and Pan stepped on the stage. *(PAN stands)*

ALL: Yea, Pan!!! *(clapping)*

PAN: Here goes! *(PAN pantomimes playing a guitar)*

SOUND: *(background music, very loud—rock guitar or country western)*

ALL: *(when music ends, crowd stomps, claps, and whistles)*
Yea!! Bravo!! Hurray!!

               (PAN sits. PAN and MIDAS give thumbs up gesture to each other)

N1:   Then Apollo took his place on stage. *(APOLLO stands)*

ALL: Yea, Apollo!!! *(clapping)*

APOLLO: Ah-hmm, Maestro. Let us begin. *(APOLLO pantomimes playing violin)*

SOUND: *(background music—Mozart, Brahms, or other soft music)*

ALL: *(when music ends, crowd stomps, claps, and whistles)*
Yea!! Bravo!! Hurray!! *(APOLLO makes a sweeping bow and sits)*

MIDAS: Attention, everyone! The contest is over, and the winner is…Pan!

ALL: Oooooh.

PAN: All right, Midas! Good choice!

APOLLO: What?!! What did you say?!!

MIDAS: Yes, indeed. No doubt about it. Pan is definitely the winner.

APOLLO: Wait just a minute. Are you saying that Pan is a better musician than I am?

MIDAS: Yes, yes, definitely better. Three cheers for Pan. Hip-hip-hooray! Hip-hip-hooray! Hip-hip-hooray! *(ALL join in on "hooray!")*

APOLLO: Midas! Something must be wrong with your ears! Perhaps you would like to listen to the music again.

MIDAS: There's nothing wrong with my ears!

APOLLO: Oh, really? We'll see about that.

N2:   Later that same day, Midas's ears began to itch.

MIDAS: *(scratching ears)* Ow, ow! Oh, oh!

N1:   He looked in the mirror and his ears were growing. They were getting long and furry.

MIDAS: Good grief! My ears! They look like donkey ears!

                                    Barbara McBride-Smith

SOUND:	Hee-haw!
N2:	King Midas pulled a hat over his ears. *(MIDAS puts on hat)*
N1:	He wore that hat all day and all night. No one, not even the queen, noticed that the king had grown donkey ears.
MIDAS:	This is very embarrassing. The world must never know.
N2:	The next day, the royal barber came to cut the king's hair.
BARBER:	Excuse me, Your Majesty, but we must remove this hat. *(BARBER pulls off MIDAS's hat)* Well, look at that! Donkey ears! Oh, my! Forgive me, sire, but you have donkey ears. *(tries to hide his laughter)*
SOUND:	*(softly)* Hee-haw.
MIDAS:	I *know* I have donkey ears! But you must forget you ever saw them. You will tell no one about my ears. Do you understand?
BARBER:	Yes, yes, Your Majesty. Of course. No one. I've forgotten already. Here's your hat...to cover your...uh...never mind. *(MIDAS puts hat on)* I suppose you won't be needing a haircut? *(laughs to himself)* Well, good day, sire. And don't worry. Your secret is safe with me.
SOUND:	*(softly)* Hee-haw.
N1:	Oh, how the barber wanted to tell somebody that secret. It was such a hard secret to keep. He thought he would burst if he didn't tell it.
N2:	The next day the barber took a very long walk. He walked out of the kingdom and through the forest until he came to a river. He dug a hole in the grass behind some reeds, and he whispered into the hole...
BARBER:	*(loud stage whisper)* The king has donkey ears.
N1:	The barber felt much better. He walked back to the kingdom, leaving the king's secret behind at the river.
N2:	The next day it rained. The grass and the reeds beside the river grew...

N1:   And grew…

N2:   And grew.

N1:   And they began to whisper:

SOUND: *(loud stage whisper)* The king has donkey ears.

N2:   The king has donkey ears.

N1:   The king has donkey ears.

ALL: The king has donkey ears. The king has donkey ears.

N1:   Meanwhile, back at the palace, King Midas was walking in his garden, when he found a satyr—

N2:   A gentle creature—half man, half horse.

N1:   The poor old satyr was sitting under a tree, looking lost and hungry.

MIDAS: Come inside, old fellow. I'll give you breakfast and a map to find your way. Then, perhaps, you'll return the favor.

N2:   King Midas knew that some satyrs could do magic.

N1:   After the satyr had eaten his fill and was ready to find his way home, he thanked the king.

SATYR: I am so grateful to you, my good King. Please allow me to grant you a wish. But mind you, I can grant only one. I'm sure there must be one thing you want more than any other.

N2:   Midas could have wished to be rid of those donkey ears…

N1:   But he didn't.

N2:   Oh, no. He was as foolish as he was greedy. He wished for gold.

MIDAS: I wish that everything I touch would turn to gold!

SATYR: Your Majesty, are you sure? Shall I forget you said that? Go on, sire. Make another wish.

MIDAS: No, no. That's my wish. I want everything I touch to turn to gold. Grant me my wish, old fellow. Now!

Barbara McBride-Smith

SATYR:	Very well, my king. But I think you'll be sorry.
MIDAS:	Sorry? Never! I love gold. Can't get enough of it.
SATYR:	Your wish is granted. Good-bye, Your Majesty. No, no, a handshake isn't necessary!
N1:	The satyr hurried out of the palace and when King Midas closed the door behind him…
SOUND:	Ping! *(hit one note on a xylophone)*
N1:	It turned to gold.
MIDAS:	Gold! Look at that! A solid gold door! I love gold!
N2:	Midas touched a chair, and…
SOUND:	Ping! *(xylophone)*
N2:	It turned to gold.
MIDAS:	A golden chair! Lovely!
N1:	He lifted a cup from the table, and…
SOUND:	Ping! *(xylophone)*
N1:	The cup turned to gold.
N2:	He tipped the cup to his lips, and…
SOUND:	Ping! *(xylophone)*
N2:	The liquid turned to gold.
MIDAS:	Blah! I love gold, but it's not very tasty for sipping.
N1:	Midas ran to his garden. He touched a rock, and…
SOUND:	Ping! *(xylophone)*
N1:	It turned to gold.
MIDAS:	Ah, ha! I can turn rocks to gold!
N2:	He picked a rose, and…
SOUND:	Ping! *(xylophone)*

N2:	It turned to gold.
MIDAS:	Magnificent!
N1:	He patted the royal dog, and…
SOUND:	Ping! *(xylophone)*
N2:	The dog turned to gold.
MIDAS:	Uh-oh, you look like a golden retriever. I'm so sorry, Rover. You looked better when you were soft and brown.
N2:	Midas reached for his handkerchief, and…
SOUND:	Ping! *(xylophone)*
N2:	It turned to gold.
MIDAS:	Now, how am I supposed to blow my nose on a golden hankie? This is really a bit too much.
N1:	He plucked an apple from a tree, and…
SOUND:	Ping! *(xylophone)*
N2:	You guessed it. It turned to gold.
MIDAS:	How am I supposed to eat or drink? What good is all this gold to me if I starve to death?
N1:	Just then, the queen walked into the garden.
MIDAS:	No, no! Stay away! Don't come near me!
N2:	Midas ran to his royal bedroom and locked himself inside. He didn't sleep very well that night, for his golden bed and golden pillow were most uncomfortable.
N1:	By morning, King Midas was sick of gold.
MIDAS:	Oh, please! Gods of Mount Olympus, take away this terrible wish! There are things in this world far more important than gold. Take it all back!
N2:	At that moment, the old satyr appeared at the king's door.

SATYR:	Midas, the Olympian gods have heard you. And they have decided to take away your golden touch. But the donkey ears… they're yours to keep. They will always remind you to be humble. Go down to the river and wash. Your golden touch will be gone.
N1:	So, King Midas ran through the forest and down to the river. He plunged into the water…
SOUND:	*(downward ripple of notes on xylophone)*
N2:	And when he came up for air…
SOUND:	*(upward ripple of notes on xylophone)*
N2:	…his golden touch *was* gone. He waded back to shore, and that was when he heard the grass and the tall reeds. They seemed to be saying…
SOUND:	*(loud stage whisper)* The king has donkey ears.
N1:	The king has donkey ears.
N2:	The king has donkey ears.
ALL:	The king has donkey ears. The king has donkey ears.
N1:	And that's how King Midas's secret became known to the whole world.
SOUND:	Ping! *(loud note on xylophone)*

Arachne and Athena

A Greek Myth

Scripted for Story Theatre by Barbara McBride-Smith

Cast of nine:
NARRATOR 1 (N1)   NEIGHBOR 1
NARRATOR 2 (N2)   NEIGHBOR 2
ARACHNE   HEPHAESTUS
ATHENA   SOUND
ZEUS

N1:   This is the story of two strong women…

ATHENA: Athena!

ARACHNE: …and Arachne!

N1:   …and their foolish pride.

ATHENA: Who are you calling foolish? Nobody can talk about a goddess like that!

ARACHNE: What do you mean pride? I'm simply *the best* weaver in the universe and everyone knows it…including her *(pointing at ATHENA)*, but she won't admit it.

ATHENA: What an ego! I am the Olympian goddess of weaving, and she *(pointing at ARACHNE)*—a mere human—dares to call herself *the best* weaver in the universe. Wait till my daddy hears about this.

N2:   Athena's father was Zeus, the chief of all the gods on Mount Olympus. He was particularly proud of Athena because she was born from his own head.

ZEUS: Oh, I'll never forget that day. I'd just eaten a rather large lunch. And quite suddenly, I got a splitting headache. I tried to take a nap, but my head felt as though it would explode. I took aspirin and herbs. I even soaked my head in salt water. But the pain only got worse. So I called my son Hephaestus to come quickly and bring his biggest hammer. *(to HEPHAESTUS)* Hit me with that hammer, Son. Right here *(pointing to head)* on top of my head.

HEPHAESTUS: *(holding hammer)* Are you sure, Pop? I might crack your skull.

ZEUS:	Yes, I'm sure! Go ahead. Hit me!
HEPHAESTUS:	Whatever you say, Pop. I always try to please. *(raises hammer)* But remember, this is gonna hurt me a lot more than it's gonna hurt you. *(lowers hammer)* Maybe you'd like to have a nice massage instead?
ZEUS:	Hit me *now*, Son!
HEPHAESTUS:	Yes, sir! *(pantomimes hitting ZEUS with hammer)*
SOUND:	*(cymbals crash)*
N2:	And you'll never believe what popped out of Zeus's head.
SOUND:	Boing! *(sound made with Vibra Slap)*
ATHENA:	Hello, Daddy! I'm your brainchild, Athena. Thanks for getting me out of your head. It was awfully crowded in there.
ZEUS:	Yes, it's true. Athena was born fully grown from my very own head.
ATHENA:	I bet I'm the best idea you ever had. Right, Dad? I'm beautiful, I'm strong, I'm intelligent, and I'm talented. What more could you want in a daughter?
N1:	But Athena was lacking one important thing…
HEPHAESTUS:	Humility! My sister has never even heard of humility. She thinks she's *the best* at everything. And she usually is.
ATHENA:	You're just jealous because Daddy made me the goddess of wisdom, war, and weaving. All you get to do is hammer away in your little blacksmith shop.
HEPHAESTUS:	Someday, Athena, you're gonna meet somebody who thinks she's as good as you are. That's a catfight I'd like to see!
ZEUS:	Sure enough, there was someone who did think she was as talented as Athena. And she was only a mortal.
N2:	Her name was Arachne. Everyone in her hometown knew who she was because she could spin and weave better than any mortal they had ever seen.
ARACHNE:	Look at all the blue ribbons I've won at the county fair for my handmade blankets and rugs. I'm unbeatable!

NEIGHBOR 1:	Arachne, who taught you how to weave like that? Has the goddess Athena been giving you lessons?
ARACHNE:	Ha! Me learn anything from that pain-in-the-head daughter of Zeus? Why, I could out-spin and out-weave Athena with my hands tied behind my back.
HEPHAESTUS:	Uh-oh. Now she's done it. Here comes the catfight.
ATHENA:	I heard that! I ought to change her into a snake-haired gorgon.
ZEUS:	Athena, I think you've already used that spell on somebody else.
ATHENA:	Oh. Right. Okay, maybe I'll just squash her like a bug. Hmmm, bug! What a brilliant idea. Time to give revenge a new look!
N1:	In a flash, Athena disguised herself as an old peddler woman. She covered up her beautiful robes with rags. She hid her golden hair under a gray wig. She pretended that she needed to walk with a cane.
N2:	Then Athena went down to Arachne's hometown. As she hobbled past Arachne's house, she stopped and called out…
ATHENA:	*(in an old woman's voice)* Hello, dear child. I've heard rumors that you insulted the great and powerful goddess Athena. She's got a mighty nasty temper. Perhaps if you apologize and ask her to forgive you, she will show you her mercy.
NEIGHBOR 2:	She's right, Arachne. It's dangerous to challenge Athena.
ARACHNE:	I'm not one bit afraid to challenge her. In fact, that's exactly what I'll do. I challenge Athena to a weaving contest! The sooner the better!
ATHENA:	You've got it, dearie. A battle of the looms—today!
N1:	Athena threw off her rags, tossed aside her cane, and straightened up to her full height of seven and a half feet.
ATHENA:	*(in ATHENA's normal voice)* I Am Athena! Goddess of weaving. I challenge you to a duel at high noon. My skill against yours. Pick your loom, mortal! Whichever of us weaves the loveliest rug by sundown is the winner.

| ARACHNE: | Athena? What a surprise! I gladly accept your challenge. Here's my loom. I'm ready! |

ARACHNE: Athena? What a surprise! I gladly accept your challenge. Here's my loom. I'm ready!

NEIGHBOR 1: *(in a loud stage whisper)* Arachne, don't do it. You can't win. She's a goddess.

ARACHNE: Of course I can win. I was born to weave.

NEIGHBOR 2: And you may *die* weaving.

ARACHNE: Athena, what will be the theme of our weavings today?

ATHENA: Let the weavings show the stories of the great gods and goddesses of Mount Olympus.

ARACHNE: Why am I not surprised? And I suppose you want your daddy Zeus to be the centerpiece of each rug?

ATHENA: Of course, the magnificent Zeus and his glorious family.

ARACHNE: Of course.

NEIGHBOR 1: Pssst! Arachne! It's not too late. Say you're sorry and back out of the contest.

ARACHNE: Never! I'm sure I can win. Let's begin.

NEIGHBOR 2: Ready. Set. Go!

N2: Athena and Arachne sat down at their looms. Their hands and shuttles began to fly through the air.

N1: They used yarns every color of the rainbow. They wove silver and gold threads into their designs.

N2: Soon pictures began to appear in their weavings.

N1: Athena's rug depicted the gods and goddesses as beautiful and kind, loved and respected by all the mortals of earth.

N2: Arachne pictured the gods and goddesses as the Twelve Stooges, slapping and bopping each other's heads and honking each other's noses.

NEIGHBOR 1: *(stage whisper)* Oh, Arachne, you are going to be in so much trouble.

ARACHNE:	*(stage whisper to her NEIGHBOR)* They're such a ridiculous family. Everyone makes fun of them. I'm the only one brave enough to admit it.
N1:	By now, the sun was setting, and a crowd had gathered around the looms. The two women completed their work and stood up.
N2:	Athena turned her loom toward the onlookers.
NEIGHBORS 1&2:	Ooooo—ahhhhhh!
N1:	Then Arachne turned her loom toward the crowd.
NEIGHBORS 1&2:	Uhhh-ohhh.
N2:	Suddenly the crowd began to snicker and giggle.
N1:	And then they began to laugh right out loud.
SOUND:	*(recording of laughter or ENTIRE CAST laughs)*
NEIGHBOR 2:	Oh Arachne, what a stitch! Your rug is beautifully woven, but you've made the gods look like nitwits.
NEIGHBOR 1:	Watch out! Here comes Athena!
ATHENA:	You miserable little mortal! How dare you show such disrespect for my family. Now you'll get what you deserve.
ARACHNE:	What I deserve is a blue ribbon.
ATHENA:	Wrong! What you deserve is the wrath of the Olympian gods. And here it comes. Get ready for a new outlook on life.
N2:	Athena picked up her wooden weaving shuttle and ran toward Arachne.
SOUND:	Whack! Whack! Whack!
N1:	Three times she hit her on her head.
NEIGHBOR 2:	Oh Arachne! Say you're sorry.
ARACHNE:	I can't. I don't know how.

N2:	Instead, Arachne ran into the woods and climbed into a tree.
N1:	Athena chased her until she found Arachne clinging to a tree limb.
ATHENA:	Well, well, you're an uppity girl, aren't you? And even I must admit that you are a skilled weaver. But you picked the wrong opponent. *Nobody* out-weaves Athena. But since you enjoy your work so much, I'm giving you the opportunity to go on doing it forever.
N2:	Athena reached into her pocket, scooped up a handful of Mount Olympus asbestos dust, and flung it over Arachne.
SOUND:	Ping! *(high note on xylophone)*
N1:	Arachne's teeth and hair fell out.
N2:	Her nose and ears and thumbs dropped off.
N1:	Her body shrank to the size of a prune.
ARACHNE:	Oh, noooooo. *(voice gets smaller and weaker)*
N1:	Arachne's eight remaining fingers changed into tiny legs. She was now...
ATHENA:	A spider! We'll call you an arachnid—the first of your species. And you'll spend the rest of your life hanging by a thread, spinning and weaving. Enjoy yourself, my dear. And remember—*never* insult a goddess!
N2:	And that's the story of...
ATHENA:	Athena!
NEIGHBOR 1:	*(pointing to ARACHNE, sadly)* And Arachne.
ZEUS:	And the battle of the looms.

Barbara McBride-Smith

Bill Erophon and His Horse Peggy Sue

A Greek Myth

Otherwise Known as Bellerophon and Pegasus
Scripted for Story Theatre by Barbara McBride-Smith

Cast of seven: NARRATOR 1 (N1)   SHERIFF IOBATES
                           NARRATOR 2 (N2)   MAYOR
                           BILL   ATHENA
                           PEGGY SUE

N1: Howdy, folks!

N2: Welcome to the Old West.

N1: Yep, the *really* Old West.

N2: Yep, this here's a story from ancient Greece.

N1: Way back yonder, long before the world ever heard tell of Pecos Bill…

N2: Or Pawnee Bill…

N1: Or Buffalo Bill…

N2: Or even ol' Wild Bill Hickock…

N1: There lived a young fella named Bill Erophon.

N2: Young Bill was a cowboy.

N1: Exceptin' he didn't have a horse.

N2: Everybody knows you can't be a real cowboy without a horse.

N1: So, here's how Bill got himself the finest horse that any cowboy ever dreamed of.

N2: Her name was Peggy Sue.

PEGGY SUE: Neigh!

N1: Bill Erophon was a handsome young buckaroo.

BILL: *(smoothing hair to indicate his good looks)* I am sooo handsome.

N2:   It was because of Bill's good looks that the mayor of Argos got jealous and accused Bill of cattle rustling.

BILL: But Mr. Mayor, I never rustled a cow in my life. Why, I don't even have a horse. All I've got is my good looks. *(smoothing hair)*

MAYOR: Well, I say you look mighty suspicious. Where else are you gettin' the money for your fancy duds and your high-priced hairdos, unless you're stealin'?

BILL: Please, Mayor sir. The only thing I've ever been guilty of stealing is the heart of any gal who looks at me. I can't help it if I am so handsome.

MAYOR: That does it! I'm sending you to Sheriff Iobates. There's nothing he likes better than hanging a cattle thief.

N1:   So, the mayor wrote a letter to Sheriff Iobates, and sent Bill Erophon to his office over at the county seat in Lycia.

MAYOR: *(pantomimes writing a letter)* Dear Sheriff Iobates, I am accusin' this fella of cattle rustlin', which is a crime. I am also accusin' him of being stuck on himself, which is an irritation. If you find him guilty on both counts, and I trust that you will, I recommend hanging him by sundown today. Yours truly, The Mayor *(folds letter and hands to SHERIFF)*

N2:   *(SHERIFF pantomimes taking letter from MAYOR and reading it)* Sheriff Iobates read the letter, but his mind wasn't on hanging anybody. He had other trouble. Big trouble. Triple trouble.

IOBATES: Oh, woe is me. How am I gonna get rid of that Chimera? It is terrorizing my territory. That monster melts, poisons, or slices and dices everything that gets close to it. I need somebody bold enough and dumb enough to go out there and whup it. *(looks at letter)* Hmmm.

BILL: Howdy, Sheriff. My name is Bill Erophon. The mayor sent me over here to see you, but I assure you that I am not guilty of stealing any cows. Everybody knows I'm a swell guy. Just ask any lady you see.

IOBATES: Are you brave, son?

Barbara McBride-Smith

BILL:	I reckon so. Why do you ask, Sheriff?
IOBATES:	Well, if you can prove to me that you are brave, I'll forget all about this letter from the mayor. In fact, if you can prove to me that you are *really* brave, I'll give you a reward—a bag of solid gold nuggets.
BILL:	A bag of solid gold nuggets! Yee-hah! You bet I'm brave, Sheriff. Just tell me what I have to do.
IOBATES:	You gotta kill the Chimera.
BILL:	What's a Chimera?
IOBATES:	It's a three-headed monster. On one end, there's a lion head that breathes fire and a goat head that has razor sharp horns. On the other end, there's a tail that bites like a poisonous serpent. Worst of all, the Chimera has a nasty attitude.
BILL:	You mean…?
IOBATES:	Yep, anything that comes within a hundred yards of its hideout is toast.
BILL:	But, what if I manage to extinguish it first?
IOBATES:	Then you get the bag of gold! Deal?
BILL:	Deal! Yee-hah! I'm gonna get rich! But wait a minute. How in the world am I gonna kill that monster? All I've got is a bow and some arrows. And my good looks. That oughta be enough. Look out Chimera. Here I come, ready or not.
N2:	Bill headed out of town.
N1:	After a while, he came to a fork in the road.
N2:	Bill had no idea which way to go. He stood there scratching his head…
N1:	When out of nowhere, a goddess appeared before him.
BILL:	Who…who are you?
ATHENA:	I am Athena, your guardian goddess. The only way you can kill the Chimera is with my help. If you can catch her, I will give you a horse. She will carry you through your battle with the Chimera.

BILL:	Are you pulling my leg? A real live horse? Yee-hah! I've always wanted a horse. I'd look especially handsome ridin' on a horse. Where is she?
ATHENA:	Take the road to the right, Bill Erophon. It will lead you to a mountain. The horse is at the top, drinking water from a stream.
BILL:	How do I catch her?
ATHENA:	Take this with you.
BILL:	What is it?
ATHENA:	It's a horse bridle, Bill. A golden horse bridle. Toss it over the horse's head, jump on her back, and hang on tight. If you can ride her until she settles down, she's yours.
BILL:	How will I know I got the right horse?
ATHENA:	Oh, you can't miss her, Bill. She's white as the snow, fast as the wind, wild as a coyote…and uh, by the way, she's got wings.
BILL:	Wings? You mean she can fly?
ATHENA:	Like a bird.
BILL:	Yippee-ti-yi-ay! A flying horse! What do I call her?
ATHENA:	By her name, of course—Peggy Sue.
BILL:	Peggy Sue, I love you!
N2:	Bill took the golden bridle, climbed the mountain, and found the beautiful winged horse drinking from a stream.
N1:	Bill tiptoed up behind Peggy Sue, threw the golden bridle over her head, leaped up on her back and hung on tight.
PEGGY SUE:	Neigh! I don't know who you are, but you don't belong on my back!
BILL:	Let's go for a ride, Peggy Sue!
PEGGY SUE:	I'll take you for a ride, all right!
N2:	Peggy Sue bucked and kicked and danced across the sky like she had dynamite in her shoes.

Barbara McBride-Smith

N1:	But Bill hung on, and at last, Peggy Sue settled down.
PEGGY SUE:	*(panting)* You sure are determined.
BILL:	Yep, I am. And I reckon you're my horse.
PEGGY SUE:	Says who?
BILL:	Athena.
PEGGY SUE:	Well, why didn't you say so in the first place? Athena and I go way back. She's my guardian goddess.
BILL:	Mine, too.
PEGGY SUE:	Then that makes us partners. And if I know Athena, she had a mighty good reason for getting us together.
BILL:	Yep. We've got to ambush a Chimera.
PEGGY SUE:	A Chimera? Why, that monster is the meanest and ugliest varmint in the West!
BILL:	That's right, Peggy Sue, and we are gonna put an end to that varmint's career.
PEGGY SUE:	If you say so, partner. I can provide the transportation. What have you got for ammunition?
BILL:	I've got my trusty bow and arrows.
PEGGY SUE:	Uh-oh. Let's hope Athena is looking out for both of us. Hang on, cowboy. Let's go kick some Chimera!
BILL:	Yee-hah!
N2:	Peggy Sue flew out over the desert. She circled while Bill looked for the Chimera's hideout.
BILL:	There it is, Peggy Sue! See that big ol' cactus with the hole beside it?
PEGGY SUE:	I see it. I also see smoke coming out of that hole.
BILL:	That's the Chimera's breath. She breathes fire, so stay out of her spittin' range. And watch out for her horns. They're sharp as razors. And don't forget that snake on her backside. It's more poisonous than a water moccasin.

PEGGY SUE: I'll take care of the flying. You take care of the shooting. Hang on, Bill. I'm going in close to see if that Chimera is home.

N1: Peggy Sue flew straight down toward the Chimera's hideout, and then hovered like a helicopter above the cactus.

N2: The Chimera heard the beating of wings and crawled out of the hole.

BILL: Hey, you low-down varmint! Look up. It's us—the dynamic duo!

N1: The Chimera growled and belched fire straight up into the air.

PEGGY SUE: Up we go! Whew, that was close.

BILL: I'll say. My boot heels are smokin'. All right, Peggy Sue. Whenever you're ready to dive again, I'll be ready to fire an arrow right between its eyes.

PEGGY SUE: Take aim, Bill. We're going in.

N2: Bill fired an arrow at the Chimera, but it bounced off without even making a nick in the Chimera's skin.

BILL: Whoo-ee. That monster's hide must be made of rubber!

PEGGY SUE: Look out! It's spitting fire and poison at the same time!

BILL: Whoa! We've got a mad monster on our hands now.

N1: Peggy Sue kept swooping and diving, staying just barely out of the Chimera's range.

N2: And Bill kept firing arrow after arrow, but every single arrow bounced off the Chimera's body and made the monster angrier.

BILL: Uh-oh. I'm down to my last arrow. Peggy Sue, what are we gonna do? *(sniffling)*

PEGGY SUE: Now, don't go getting soft on me, partner. You're a real cowboy. I'm sure you'll think up a sure-fire plan.

BILL: I'm thinkin', I'm thinkin'. Uhhhh…OK! I got a plan. Where's my lariat?

N1: Bill pulled the lead arrowhead off the shaft of his last arrow. He tied it to the end of his lariat.

N2:   Peggy Sue made a dive right for the Chimera's lion head, and Bill lassoed the lion's tongue.

N1:   When the Chimera spit fire from its mouth, the fire melted the arrowhead.

N2:   The hot, molten lead trickled down its throat and scorched the monster's insides.

BILL: Ohhh, that's gotta hurt. Listen to it scream.

PEGGY SUE: You did it, Bill! You got it!

N1:   The Chimera rolled over, stuck its legs in the air, and belched one last puff of smoke.

BILL: Yippee! The Chimera is dead! Let's go tell Sheriff Iobates the good news.

N2:   Bill and Peggy Sue flew non-stop to Lycia, and the whole town turned out to welcome them back as heroes.

IOBATES: Congratulations, Bill Erophon. You are a hero. I reckon I won't have to hang you after all. And here's your bag of gold.

N1:   Bill bought himself a ranch and a lot of fancy clothes. He had his hair styled every week.

BILL: I *do* look good. Yep, that's me—a good-lookin' hero. And I'm rich, to boot.

N2:   As time went by, Bill's ego got bigger and bigger.

BILL: I'm so famous, I ought to be hanging out with the gods of Mount Olympus.

PEGGY SUE: Better watch it, Bill. Your head's so big, it probably won't fit in your ten-gallon hat anymore.

BILL: I bet Athena still remembers me. I think I'll just fly up to Mount Olympus and have dinner with Athena and her daddy, Zeus.

PEGGY SUE: You can't go to Mount Olympus without an invitation, Bill.

BILL: Sure I can. The gods love handsome heroes. Get your best saddle on, Peggy Sue. We're flying up there tonight.

N1:	Bill pointed Peggy Sue's nose into the air, and off they flew toward Mount Olympus.
N2:	At that very moment, Athena just happened to look down and see them coming.
ATHENA:	Daddy, come look at this! It's that boy Bill Erophon. He's coming up here without an invitation. You always said he was gonna get too big for his britches.
N1:	Zeus grabbed a thunderbolt and flung it at Bill. It hit him right between the eyes and knocked him off Peggy Sue.
BILL:	Helllllllllp! *(loud to soft, as if falling)*
N2:	Bill fell down, down, down from the sky and landed on a giant cactus in the desert.
N1:	Bill was so bruised and scarred, he never went home or showed his face in public again.
N2:	He wandered, down and out, for many years. He died a lonely and forgotten hero in the hills of Delphi.
PEGGY SUE:	I had a happier ending than poor ol' Bill. Zeus allowed me to fly on up to Mount Olympus. He gave me my own personal stall and all the honey granola I could eat. Whenever Zeus went on a trip, I carried his thunderbolts. But I never had to carry another cowboy on my back again.
ATHENA:	And when Peggy Sue got too old to strut her stuff anymore, Daddy Zeus changed her into a constellation of stars and gave her a place in the sky.
N1:	And she's still up there. If you know where to look, maybe you can see her coming over the horizon.
N2:	She's still bucking and kicking and dancing like she's got dynamite in her shoes.

Barbara McBride-Smith

Atalanta

A Greek Myth

Scripted for Story Theatre by Barbara McBride-Smith

Cast of seven:

NARRATOR 1 (N1)	ARTEMIS
NARRATOR 2 (N2)	APHRODITE
ATALANTA	KING
HIPPOMENES	

N1: Atalanta was a *girl!*

N2: Yes. So?

N1: Her father wanted a boy. You know, a son.

N2: Why?

N1: In ancient Greece, a king needed a son for an heir.

N2: A daughter couldn't be an heir?

N1: Well, King Iasus didn't think so. And when Atalanta was born, he ordered his servants to leave the girl-child on a hillside to die.

N2: And that's when the gods of Mount Olympus showed up in the story. Let me guess. Was it Athena?

N1: Not this time.

N2: Was it Aphrodite?

N1: She showed up later.

N2: Must have been Artemis.

N1: You got it. Artemis, goddess of the hunt, found the sleeping baby abandoned on a hillside and sent a mother bear to look after the child.

N2: The mother bear warmed Atalanta with her own furry body and nursed her with her own milk.

N1: Years went by. The child grew strong and lived as if she were a bear cub.

N2:   One day, a band of hunters saw the little girl playing near the bear cave. They waited until the mother bear left the cave. Then they kidnapped Atalanta and took her home with them.

N1:   Atalanta grew up in a family of many sons. She was taught how to hunt and run and wrestle as well as any boy.

N2:   You can imagine her surprise when, one day, the goddess Artemis told her who she really was.

ARTEMIS: Atalanta, I know this will come as a surprise. But you are a princess.

ATALANTA: A princess? That's impossible! I never wear dresses, and certainly not glass slippers. I don't know how to dance or spin gold, or whatever it is that princesses do. And I don't like pink! I am a hunter!

ARTEMIS: Oh yes, you are a fine hunter…and one of the swiftest runners I've ever seen. I've been watching you, and I've secretly guided you in your training.

ATALANTA: Really? Could I join your band of nymphs and hunt with you? Please, let me come with you, Artemis.

ARTEMIS: Maybe someday, Atalanta. But for now, you must return to your father, King Iasus, and prove to him that you are more than equal to any son he might have had.

ATALANTA: But if my father didn't want me when I was born, why would he accept me now?

ARTEMIS: Someday you could be the mother of a son—his grandson. Your father will believe that you are his only hope for an heir.

ATALANTA: Never! I'll never marry or have children. I want to be just like you, Artemis—free to run and hunt as I choose. I don't want a husband.

ARTEMIS: Then return to your father and claim your rights as his heir. Prove to him that he was wrong to discard you when you were born a daughter instead of a son.

N1:   So Atalanta returned to the palace where she had been born. Many of the servants knew who she was. They took Atalanta to King Iasus.

Barbara McBride-Smith

ATALANTA: Father, I'll bet you never expected to see me again. I've changed, haven't I?

KING: Well, well, look at you. It's little…what was it your mother named you? Atlas-Ann?

ATALANTA: Ata-lanta. She named me Atalanta.

KING: Ah yes, that was it. So sad about your mother. She died not long after…uh, after you went away.

ATALANTA: Yes, Father. I heard. You thought she would have sons to replace me, but I am your only child. And now I have returned so that you may give me my rightful place as your heir.

KING: Hmmm…Spunky girl, aren't you?

ATALANTA: Yes. Also strong and smart.

KING: My servants tell me that you are a wrestling champion, a famous huntress, and a gold medal contender in track and field. If that's all true, you're almost as good as a son.

ARTEMIS: He will soon see that she is equal to any son!

N2:   And so it was that Atalanta came home to live with her father.

N1:   But Atalanta didn't act like a princess, and her father grew weary of her.

KING: Atlas-Ann, dear…

ATALANTA: Ata-lanta, Father.

KING: Yes, yes, Ata-lanta. Whatever. It's time we found a husband for you.

ATALANTA: But Father, I don't want a husband.

KING: Of course you want a husband, silly girl. If you have a husband, then you can have a son. And if you have a son, I will have a grandson!

ATALANTA: Father, you're not listening. I don't want a husband or a child. Not now. Maybe someday, maybe not.

KING: And you are not listening, my dear. Without a son, you will never inherit my throne.

ARTEMIS:	He still doesn't get it. We'll just have to teach him a lesson. Here's the plan. *(leans over and whispers something to ATALANTA)*
N2:	Atalanta agreed, at last, to find a husband.
KING:	Oh goody! *(clapping his hands)*
ATALANTA:	But there are two conditions.
KING:	Yes? Name them.
ATALANTA:	I will marry any man who can outrun me in a footrace.
KING:	Well, that should be easy enough.
ARTEMIS:	Ha! Wait till he sees her run.
ATALANTA:	*and*...any man who races against me and loses...will also lose his head.
KING:	Nice touch, dear. That should narrow the applicants to the bravest and fastest. That's exactly the sort of husband you'll want.
N1:	In spite of this dangerous condition, many men came to challenge Atalanta in a race.
N2:	They thought it would be easy to outrun a girl.
ARTEMIS:	Look at them. Each suitor goes to the starting point with a smile on his face.
N1:	But Atalanta ran like the wind, and no one reached the finishing post ahead of her.
N2:	Many men paid the penalty for losing the race by losing their heads.
N1:	And still, suitors came to try their luck.
ARTEMIS:	How foolish they are! She's unbeatable.
N2:	And then, one day a young man arrived to watch Atalanta run.
N1:	His name was Hippomenes. He was a very good runner, but he had no intentions of racing against Atalanta. He wanted only to see for himself "the fastest woman on earth."

Barbara McBride-Smith

HIPPOMENES: Look at her go! She's amazing! I wonder if she would teach me how to be a stronger runner. I'll talk to her father about meeting her.

KING: So, you want my daughter to be your coach? Perhaps she'll agree. But first, she'll want to see you run. Go ahead and race against her.

HIPPOMENES: Isn't there some other way to talk to her?

KING: Sorry. You're not afraid to race a girl, are you?

HIPPOMENES: To tell you the truth, sir, *yes*. I am afraid. She's faster than anything on two feet—except for the goddess Artemis.

ARTEMIS: Oh, I *do* like this boy!

KING: Tell you what. Enter the race. If you can even come close to beating my daughter to the finish line, I'll personally see to it that you keep your head. *(to himself)* Heh, heh. You might have to keep it in your back pocket, but maybe you'll get lucky and win.

ARTEMIS: Uh-oh. Hippomenes is in trouble. He needs some goddess assistance. My loyalty is to Atalanta, but maybe one of my sisters will help. Hmmm. Aphrodite! Can we talk?

APHRODITE: Yes, Artemis. I've seen what's happening. I'll be glad to help that lovely couple.

N2: Aphrodite went out to her garden and picked three golden apples. Then she appeared to Hippomenes and gave him the apples.

APHRODITE: Use these as I tell you, and you will win the race. Don't worry. I'm on your side.

N1: On the day of the race, Hippomenes arrived at the track with the three golden apples hidden in his tunic.

ARTEMIS &
APHRODITE: Ready. Set. Go!

N2: At the signal, the two runners were off.

N1: For the first lap, Atalanta and Hippomenes were side by side.

N2:	But when Atalanta began to pull ahead of Hippomenes, he tossed one of the golden apples onto the track in front of her.
ATALANTA:	What was that?
N1:	Atalanta stopped long enough to pick up the golden apple.
ATALANTA:	How beautiful! Must be a sign from Artemis. Or could it be…? Oops, he's ahead!
N2:	Atalanta tucked the apple into her tunic and dashed ahead of Hippomenes.
HIPPOMENES:	Here goes apple number two.
ATALANTA:	There's another one! I can't leave it here.
N1:	Atalanta stopped to pick up the second apple.
ATALANTA:	Why is this happening?
N2:	And again, Hippomenes passed her by.
ATALANTA:	No time to think. Gotta run!
N1:	Atalanta tucked away the apple and shot ahead of Hippomenes.
HIPPOMENES:	She's even faster than I imagined! Here's my last hope. Aphrodite, please don't fail me now.
N2:	Hippomenes threw the third apple in Atalanta's path. She stopped and picked it up.
ATALANTA:	These apples—they must be messages from the goddesses. But what do they mean? Why can't I resist them? Are they enchanted? Why am I standing here asking questions when I should be running?
N1:	Indeed, Aphrodite had cast a spell on those apples. Atalanta had no choice but to pick them up.
N2:	And while she was pondering the apples, Hippomenes won the race.
KING:	Hurray! He won! He won! Atalanta has found herself a husband!

ARTEMIS: Aphrodite, it wasn't supposed to turn out this way! It was supposed to be a tie! Then Atalanta could choose for herself what to do about Hippomenes. You didn't play *fair!*

APHRODITE: *All* is fair in love and war. This is both. Besides, my team always wins. You should have known that when you asked me to help.

ARTEMIS: But Atalanta doesn't want to marry Hippomenes!

APHRODITE: Maybe not. But with those three golden apples in the bank, she can get away from her father. He's the real loser. Hippomenes is a winner.

ARTEMIS: Whether he wins Atalanta's heart remains to be seen. I say she'll run free, like me, for the rest of her life.

APHRODITE: I wouldn't bet on it.

N1:   And how did it all turn out? Well, Atalanta did leave her father's kingdom.

N2:   And eventually she and Hippomenes did marry.

N1:   But they were so busy running races and trying to grow golden apples from seeds, they forgot to thank the goddesses who helped them.

APHRODITE: No songs, no praises, no offerings at our temples! What are they thinking?

ARTEMIS: Neglect of a goddess is dangerous.

N2:   Aphrodite and Artemis changed Atalanta and Hippomenes into lions and harnessed them to a chariot driven by the grandmother of the gods.

N1:   So Atalanta, who wanted so much to run free, became a captive for the rest of her days.

N2:   Such is the irony of the gods.

Demeter and Persephone

A Greek Myth

Scripted for Story Theatre by Barbara McBride-Smith

Cast of six:

NARRATOR 1 (N1)	DEMETER
NARRATOR 2 (N2)	PERSEPHONE
HADES	ZEUS

N1: Long ago...

N2: the Greeks say,

N1: ...twelve gods lived on Mount Olympus and ruled the universe.

ZEUS: Uh, pardon the interruption, but that's not exactly accurate.

N1: Oh really? And who are you?

ZEUS: I'm Zeus, the head of the Olympian family. You see, only ten of the original Olympians lived on Mount Olympus.

N2: Who was missing?

ZEUS: First, there was my brother Poseidon.

N1: Oh right! Poseidon, the god of the sea.

ZEUS: And then, there was my other brother.

N2: You mean...Hades?

ZEUS: Yes, Hades. He always was the black sheep of the family. When we took power on Mount Olympus, I offered him his own piece of land—a place where he could build his own kingdom. But he said it was too bright and breezy on Mount Olympus. He wanted some place dark and hot.

N1: And that's why he decided to live under the earth?

ZEUS: Yes, he built his own underworld kingdom. It wasn't a pretty sight.

N2: And no one else lived there with him?

ZEUS:	Not at first. But after a while, the family decided he needed some company, so we began to send the dead spirits of mortals down to his underworld. It was strange, but he seemed to enjoy being in charge of corpses.
N1:	Oh yes, now I remember. He lived among the dead for many years. And then, he became lonely and wanted a wife.
N2:	A dead mortal would never do as a wife for a god.
ZEUS:	Certainly not! And so Hades went looking for a Queen of the Underworld.
N1:	Demeter, goddess of the harvest, had a beautiful young daughter named Persephone.
N2:	Demeter loved her daughter dearly and almost never let the girl out of her sight.
ZEUS:	But one day…
PERSEPHONE:	Mom, please may I go with my friends to the meadow to pick some flowers? I won't be gone long.
DEMETER:	Oh, my darling Persephone, you know how I worry when you're away from me. This world is a dangerous place for a child.
PERSEPHONE:	But Mom, I'm not a child any more! I've grown up. Please let me spend the afternoon with my friends. We'll be perfectly safe together.
DEMETER:	I suppose you're right. You are a young woman now. Promise you'll be very careful?
PERSEPHONE:	Yes, I'll be very careful.
DEMETER:	And remember, never talk to strangers.
PERSEPHONE:	Of course, Mom. Never, never, never.
DEMETER:	Stay close to your friends, dear. And don't go into the woods.
PERSEPHONE:	Stop worrying, Mom. I'll be fine. I'll bring you a bouquet of wildflowers. You love flowers, don't you? See you later. I'll be home in time to help with dinner.

N1:	Persephone and her friends ran down to the meadow. They danced and sang and gathered flowers all afternoon.
N2:	Demeter went about her chores, trying not to worry about her child. But of course, she did worry.
N1:	Meanwhile, down in the underworld, Hades was looking through his periscope at the upper world.
N2:	He often entertained himself by observing the adventures of the mortals and immortals who lived above him.
HADES:	Egads! Look at that! What a beautiful young woman! Hmmm, I've been feeling a bit lonely lately. A wife would be a fine addition to my kingdom. That's it! I'll make that young woman my Queen of the Underworld.
ZEUS:	Wait just a minute, Hades! I heard that! That girl is the daughter of an Olympian goddess. You can't go kidnapping her right out from under my nose.
HADES:	Why not? She doesn't already have a husband, does she? What woman wouldn't want her daughter to be a queen?
ZEUS:	Demeter, that's who! She loves that girl more than anything. And she has no intentions of letting her marry anyone— especially you!
HADES:	Tell you what, big brother. Let's make a deal. You let me take Persephone home with me, and I'll have my friends the Cyclopes make you a brand new set of golden thunderbolts. Then you tell Demeter that her daughter ran off to be a movie star. Whaddya say?
ZEUS:	Golden thunderbolts, huh? Ooooh, I've always wanted a set of those. Can you decorate them with diamonds and rubies?
HADES:	Sure! Whatever makes you happy, brother.
ZEUS:	It might just work. Demeter is gonna be furious, of course. She'll probably throw a fit. But she'll get over it. What bad could happen?
HADES:	So, it's a deal?
ZEUS:	Deal! Persephone is yours. I'll handle Demeter.

HADES: Yes!

N1: Back at the meadow, Persephone was looking for some special flowers to bring her mother.

N2: Suddenly, she heard a loud cracking sound, and the earth split open right before her eyes.

PERSEPHONE: Help! An earthquake!

HADES: No, my dear, it's only me—your husband-to-be, Hades!

N1: At that moment, a black chariot drawn by a dozen black horses climbed out of the earth.

N2: Hades reached out to grab Persephone.

HADES: Come with me, you lovely thing. We'll be married today.

PERSEPHONE: No! Get away from me! My mother told me not to talk to strangers. I'm certain she wouldn't want me marrying one.

HADES: Your mother will just have to get used to the idea. You're the lucky girl I've chosen to be my Queen of the Underworld. Time to go now. All aboard!

N1: Hades seized Persephone, pulled her into his chariot, and drove with her back down under the earth.

PERSEPHONE: Helllllp! Helllllp! Mom, where are you?

N2: Demeter was home, watching the clock. It was dinnertime, the sun was setting…

N1: and Persephone wasn't home yet.

DEMETER: Oh, I knew I shouldn't have let her go anywhere without me. Something terrible must have happened. I'd better get down to that meadow and see if she has wandered into the woods and gotten lost. Or maybe she's broken a leg and can't walk home.

N2: Demeter ran down to the meadow, and there was Zeus sitting on a tree stump. He had already sent Persephone's friends home with instructions to tell no one what had really happened.

ZEUS:	Demeter, how nice to see you! I know you'll be disappointed to hear this, but Persephone has run away from home. She said something about being a...uhh...an underground film star. Yes, that was it. I tried to stop her, but she was determined. She asked me to tell you not to worry. She'll be in touch.
DEMETER:	My Persephone? Run away from home? Not in a million years! She's a good girl. She has never caused me a moment of trouble, and she wouldn't go anywhere without asking me first. There must be some other explanation. What's going on, Zeus?!
ZEUS:	Uhhh, well I hate to break your heart, Demeter, but I suspect that Persephone has fallen in love and eloped with the man of her nightmares...uh, the man of her dreams. I'm sure she'll be very happy.
DEMETER:	Zeus, you've never been very good at lying. You're covering up something. You know exactly what happened to my daughter, and you're afraid to tell me. Now, *where is she?!!*
ZEUS:	Demeter, I'd love to stay and chat, but I really must get back to the mountain. Come see me when you've calmed down a bit.
DEMETER:	Zeus, I *will* get to the bottom of this. If you're involved in any way with my daughter's disappearance, I'll make your life miserable until I get her back safe and sound.
N1:	After weeks of searching and asking questions, Demeter learned the truth.
N2:	Persephone had been kidnapped by Hades and taken to the underworld.
DEMETER:	Zeus! I know where my daughter is! Her friends told me what happened. You get her back to me *now!*
ZEUS:	Oh Demeter, just settle down and look on the bright side. Your daughter is married to a god. She's Queen of the Underworld. I heard it was a lovely wedding. Perhaps you can go for a visit sometime.
DEMETER:	I want my daughter back! Do you hear me? I'm mad, and I'm not gonna take this anymore!
ZEUS:	Uh-oh, if Mama ain't happy, ain't nobody happy.

| DEMETER: | That's right! I've got power, and I'll use it. Until my daughter comes home, nothing is going to grow on this earth! Nothing! No corn, no wheat, no flowers, no tomatoes, no zucchini! The ground is gonna be cold and barren. Even a lizard won't be able to survive. So, sit up there in your palace and watch what happens. Very soon, you'll be god of a dustbowl! |

DEMETER: That's right! I've got power, and I'll use it. Until my daughter comes home, nothing is going to grow on this earth! Nothing! No corn, no wheat, no flowers, no tomatoes, no zucchini! The ground is gonna be cold and barren. Even a lizard won't be able to survive. So, sit up there in your palace and watch what happens. Very soon, you'll be god of a dustbowl!

N1: Demeter kept her promise. Everything on the earth stopped growing.

N2: Everything green turned yellow.

N1: And the yellow turned brown.

N2: The crops died, and the birds stopped singing.

N1: The earth became dusty and cold and barren.

ZEUS: *(holding a telephone)* Hades, have you seen what's going on up here? Demeter is turning this place into Siberia. I didn't know how much power she could muster up. Listen, we may have to cut a deal with her.

HADES: *(holding a telephone)* If you think the earth looks bad, you ought to see Persephone. She hasn't eaten a bite of food since she's been here. She's nothing but skin and bones. The corpses down here look better than my bride!

ZEUS: Tell you what, you get her to eat something, she'll feel better, she'll look better, and you'll get to keep her…well, at least on a part time basis. Try offering her a pomegranate. She's never been able to resist a juicy pomegranate.

HADES: And if she doesn't eat it?

ZEUS: Then it's back to her mother she goes. *(puts down telephone)*

HADES: *(puts down telephone)* Oh, Persephone dear, look what I've got for you! *(pantomimes holding out a pomegranate)* A fresh juicy pomegranate. Have a bite. It'll taste so sweet. Go on. What bad could happen?

PERSEPHONE: No, I can't. I promised myself I wouldn't eat anything until you let me go home to my mother. But I'm soooo hungry. Well, maybe just a few seeds. *(pantomimes eating three seeds)* Yum! Delicious! *(eats three more seeds)*

N2:	By eating those six pomegranate seeds, Persephone sealed the deal.
ZEUS:	Persephone, the Fates have decided. You may return to your mother…but only for half the year. For the other six months, you will live with your husband in the underworld.
N1:	So, for half of every year, Persephone stayed with Demeter. *(DEMETER and PERSEPHONE put arms over each other's shoulders)*
PERSEPHONE:	Oh, Mom, it's good to be home.
DEMETER:	I've missed you so much, Persephone. To celebrate your return, I'll make the earth beautiful again.
N2:	Demeter was happy, and it was spring and summer.
N1:	But, for half of every year, Persephone went back to live with Hades.
HADES:	*(taking PERSEPHONE's hand)* Welcome home, my queen. I've been lonely here without you.
N2:	Hades was happy…
N1:	But Demeter grieved, and the earth became cold and barren again…
N2:	And it was fall and winter.
N1:	And that's the way the world has been ever since.
DEMETER:	Remember this story when you see the seasons change…
PERSEPHONE:	Spring and summer…
HADES:	Fall and winter…
N2:	Persephone still comes and goes between two worlds.

The Twelve Labors of Hercules
A Greek Myth

Scripted for Story Theatre by Barbara McBride-Smith

Cast of fifteen:
NARRATOR 1 (N1)	HERCULES
NARRATOR 2 (N2)	KING
HERA	SOUND
NINE KING'S ASSISTANTS (KA1, KA2, ETC.)	

N1: Long ago in Greece, a princess named Alcmene gave birth to a baby boy—a very *big* baby boy. He was three times the size of a normal child.

N2: This was the biggest baby anybody in Greece had ever seen. But he was also one of the most beautiful babies anybody had ever seen.

N1: His mother named him Hercules, which means "earth's glory." She couldn't stop admiring her huge, healthy son.

N2: But there was someone else who admired Hercules—the goddess Hera on Mount Olympus. But her admiration was full of jealousy.

HERA: Look at the size of that baby! He's bigger and more handsome than any of *my* children! I suppose I'll have to send a little accident his way.

N1: Suddenly a gigantic deadly snake crawled into the cradle where Hercules was sleeping.

SOUND: Sssssssssss.

HERCULES: Goo! Gaa! Oooo, wook at dat snake. Snake got big forked tongue. Uh-oh, snake gonna bite wittle me. Haiiiiiii! *(karate chops snake)*

SOUND: Whack! *(two pieces of wood clap together—making chopping noise)*

HERCULES: Bye-bye, snake.

N2: Hercules was so powerful, Hera could never find a way to harm him. So he grew to be a strong young man.

HERCULES: I'm all grown up now. It's time I found a wife and had a family of my own.

N1:   Hercules married a princess named Megera, and they had three fine sons.

HERCULES: Come on, boys, I'll teach you how to karate chop a snake. You never know when it might come in handy.

N2:   Meanwhile, Hera was watching Hercules from Mount Olympus. She was still jealous. And she was still plotting a way to destroy him.

HERA: Look at him. He's so happy with his perfect little family. None of *my* children ever look that happy. Hmmm, I wonder what would happen if I put an evil spell on him and he did some terrible deed. Then he wouldn't be so perfect anymore!

N1:   Hera cast a spell over Hercules that made him go stark raving mad.

HERA: Double, double, toil and trouble.

HERCULES: Helllllp! I'm being attacked by snakes! They're all over me! I must destroy them. Haiiiiii!

SOUND: Whack! Whack! Whack! Whack! *(wooden blocks clack together four times)*

N2:   When Hercules came to his senses again, he discovered that he had killed his wife and three young sons.

HERCULES: Oh noooo! How could I have done such a horrible thing? Please, gods of Mount Olympus, turn me into a madman again. I would rather be crazy than live with this guilt and sadness.

HERA: Oh, poor dear Hercules. The gods of Olympus will forgive you if you perform twelve tasks for King Eurystheus of Tiryns.

HERCULES: Yes, anything. I'll do whatever he asks.

N1:   So Hercules traveled for many miles until he came to the palace of King Eurystheus.

KING: *Zzzzzzz. (loud snoring)*

HERA:	Eurystheus! Wake up, you evil pig-faced king! A very strong young man is waiting outside your palace. Invite him in. He is under a curse, and I am putting him in your service for twelve years. You may ask him to do twelve tasks. And he will do them no matter how difficult. Have fun!
SOUND:	Knock-knock! *(knocking on door)*
KING:	Come in, come in. So, you're the great Hercules? And you've come to do twelve labors for me, eh? Excellent! Here's a shopping list for you. Assistants, help me out. Hercules, here's what I want.
KA1:	Nine animals.
KA2:	One monster.
KA3:	A few golden apples.
KA4:	And one pair of underwear.
SOUND:	Boiiinnng! *(funny noise as made by a Vibra Slap)*
KING:	Easy, huh? So, get going.
HERCULES:	Uh, Your Majesty. About that list…could you be more specific?
KING:	Certainly, more specifically *you're* going to get for *me*…
KA1:	One feline. *(holds up sign that says* FELINE*)*
SOUND:	Meow!
KA2:	One equine. *(sign—*EQUINE*)*
SOUND:	Neigh! *(horse whinny)*
KA3:	One porcine. *(sign—*PORCINE*)*
SOUND:	Oink-oink!
KA4:	Three bovines. *(sign—*3 BOVINES*)*
SOUND:	Mooooo!
KA5:	One canine. *(sign—*CANINE*)*
SOUND:	Woof! Woof!

KA6:	One serpentine. *(sign—*SERPENTINE*)*
SOUND:	Sssss!
KA7:	The birds. *(sign—*BIRDS*)*
SOUND:	Caw! Caw!
KA8:	The apples. *(sign—*APPLES*)*
SOUND:	Yum-yum!
KA9:	The deer. *(sign—*DEER*)*
SOUND:	*(singing)* Rudolph the red-nosed...
KING:	And don't forget the underwear! *(sign—*UNDERWEAR*)*
SOUND:	Boiiinnng! *(funny noise as made by a Vibra Slap)*
HERCULES:	Wait a minute. Wait just a minute. How am I supposed to remember all of that, Your Majesty?
KING:	Your body may be very strong, oh mighty Hercules, but your memory is very weak. We'll tell you again, and this time *pay attention* and *take notes!* Here we go.
KA1:	One feline. *(holds up sign that says* FELINE*)*
N1:	You must kill the great Nemean lion.
KING:	And watch out, his teeth and claws are like razors.
HERCULES:	Task number one: Kill the big lion. *(as he repeats each task, he pretends to be writing a list)* OK, what's next?
KA2:	One equine. *(sign—*EQUINE*)*
N2:	You must capture the horses of King Diomedes.
KING:	Oh, I should mention that these are man-eating horses.
HERCULES:	Number two: Capture the man-eating horses. *(continues to make list)* Next?
KA3:	One porcine. *(sign—*PORCINE*)*
N1:	Catch the giant wild boar in the forest.

KING: Be sure to bring it back to me *alive,* my dear boy.

HERCULES: Catch a pig. Okie-dokie.

KA4: Three bovines. *(sign*—3 BOVINES*)*

N2: *(holds up one finger)* Clean the filthy cattle barn of King Augeas. *(holds up two fingers)* Fetch an ogre's cows. *(holds up three fingers)* And capture the white bull of Crete.

KING: Oh Hercules, you might want to put a few warnings in your notes: The cattle barn of King Augeas hasn't been cleaned out in thirty years. It stinks! The ogre named Geryon has three heads, carries a big stick, and he loves his cows. And as for the white bull of Crete, he breathes fire through his nostrils.

HERCULES: Clean barn. Steal cows. Capture bull. Got it!

KA5: One canine. *(sign*—CANINE*)*

N1: Bring the dog named Cerberus back from Hades' underworld.

KING: Oh, did I mention that Cerberus has three heads? That means three sets of teeth. And they're very long and sharp.

HERCULES: Fetch the unfriendly dog. OK. What else?

KA6: One serpentine. *(sign*—SERPENTINE*)*

N2: Destroy the nine-headed Hydra.

KING: Biggest snake you've ever laid eyes on, Hercules. And each of its nine heads spits poison. And if you cut off one head, two new heads will grow in its place.

HERCULES: Waste the Hydra. Watch out for multiplying heads. Next?

KA7: The birds. *(sign*—BIRDS*)*

N1: Chase away a flock of flesh-eating birds.

KING: Very big birds, Hercules. Very hungry birds. Their wings, beaks, and claws are made of brass. And they're always in a bad mood.

HERCULES: Scatter the birds and run fast. Check.

KA8:	The apples. *(sign—APPLES)*
N2:	Gather three golden apples from the Tree of the Hesperides.
KING:	Ah, yes. The magic tree at the end of the Earth. A ferocious dragon is guarding the tree. And only the giant Atlas is allowed within a hundred feet of those apples. Unfortunately, Atlas is busy holding up the sky. What a pity.
HERCULES:	Hmmm. Trick Atlas into picking the golden apples. Next?
KA9:	The deer. *(sign—DEER)*
N1:	Bring to the palace the stag with the golden antlers.
KING:	Let me assure you, Hercules. This is the fastest and most beautiful deer you've ever seen. The goddess Artemis loves this deer so much she has vowed to kill anyone who hurts it.
HERCULES:	Borrow the stag and be nice to Artemis. OK. And the last task, Your Majesty?
KING:	The underwear! *(sign—UNDERWEAR)*
HERCULES:	Underwear? Whose underwear?
N2:	The golden girdle worn by the queen of the Amazons.
KING:	And she never takes it off. Never.
HERCULES:	Amazon underwear. That makes twelve, Your Majesty.
KING:	Yes, it does, my boy. Now we'll run the list by you one more time to be sure you haven't left anything out. All right, everybody, quick summary of the Twelve Labors.
KA3:	Try to capture the big old hog. *(sign—PORCINE)*
KA5:	Bring back from Hades the three-headed dog. *(sign—CANINE)*
KA4:	Fetch two of the three bovine herds. *(sign—3 BOVINES)*
KA7:	Chase away the big ugly birds. *(sign—BIRDS)*
KA6:	Kill the many-headed snake. *(sign—SERPENTINE)*
KA4:	Clean up after the other beefsteak. *(sign—3 BOVINES)*

KA9:	The big deer lives. *(sign*—DEER*)*
KA1:	Big lion has to die. *(sign*—FELINE*)*
KA8:	Don't use the golden apples to make a nice pie. *(sign*—APPLES*)*
KA2:	You must put a stop to the man-eating mares. *(sign*—EQUINE*)*
N1 & N2:	And don't forget the underwear!! *(sign*—UNDERWEAR*)*
KING:	Got it?
HERCULES:	Got it!
ALL KAs:	Good!
HERA:	Yoo-hoo, Hercules! Good luck!
KING:	Make it snappy, Hercules. I'll be waiting.
HERCULES:	Twelve Labors, here I come. And, Your Majesty… *(using "Terminator" voice) I'll be back!*

The Contest for Athens

A Greek Myth

Scripted for Story Theatre by Barbara McBride-Smith

Cast of fourteen: DEITIES (D1, D2, D3, D4, D5, D6, D7)
                     NARRATOR 1 (N1)   ATHENA
                     NARRATOR 2 (N2)   ARES
                     ZEUS   DEMETER
                     POSEIDON

N1: A few thousand years ago, the gods and goddesses of Mount Olympus had a land run.

N2: The whole thing started because some of the deities were arguing about which parts of the earth were their patron territories.

D1: I'll take California!

D2: No, you take Texas, and I'll take California.

D3: I already claimed Texas!

D4: How about if we split Texas down the middle and you each get half?

D5: While ya'll are arguing about Texas, I'm taking Alaska!

D6: Not fair! If you get Alaska, I get New York, Hawaii, and Florida!

D7: Who wants New Jersey? *(silence; other DEITIES shake heads)* Aw, come on! Somebody's gotta take New Jersey.

D2: Why? Nobody took Oklahoma.

D4: Or Kansas.

D3: Forget the small potatoes! What do we do with the South Pole?

N1: Finally, Zeus got tired of the bargaining and bickering and came up with a solution.

ZEUS: *(blows whistle)* Listen up, everybody! We're gonna have a land run. Line up right here. And no cheating! At the sound of my thunderbolt, you can start running. Choose whatever territory you want and register your claim with my office. Everybody understand the rules?

D1:	Is flying allowed?
ZEUS:	No, Hermes. No flying. This is called a land *run*. Get it?
D1:	OK, Boss. Just checking.
ZEUS:	On your mark…get set… *(cymbals crash)* GO!
N2:	It looked as though the race was a grand success.
N1:	Until a fight broke out between Athena and Poseidon.
POSEIDON:	It's mine!
ATHENA:	No way!
POSEIDON:	Yes way! I got here first!
ATHENA:	Did not!
POSEIDON:	Did, too!
ATHENA:	I'm building a city on this land, and I'm naming it after myself!
POSEIDON:	Oh yeah? You and what army?
N2:	Zeus knew that Athena and Poseidon were as stubborn as a pair of cross-eyed mules, so he had to get tough.
ZEUS:	Chill out, both of you! We'll find a way to settle this in a civilized manner.
POSEIDON:	Right! A duel at sunrise!
ARES:	Great idea! I'll supply the weapons.
ATHENA:	Too dull. Let's have a debate. A political-type debate.
POSEIDON:	Nah, too nasty. Let's just mud-wrestle for this piece of land.
ZEUS:	No, forget all that stuff. Debates and mud-slinging are too common. The sort of things humans do. What we need is a dignified contest.
DEMETER:	Yes. Let us be dignified.
D5:	Three cheers for dignified! Hip-hip…
ALL:	Hooray!

Barbara McBride-Smith

D5:	Hip-hip…
ALL:	Hooray!
D5:	Hip-hip…
ALL:	Hooray!
ARES:	Go ahead, Chief. Give us your brilliant, dignified idea.
POSEIDON:	We're all ears.
ATHENA:	Name the terms. I'll take him on!
ZEUS:	Athena…Poseidon…Each of you will present to this future city a gift. Something special. The rest of us will vote to determine which of you has given the best gift. Whoever wins gets it all—lock, stock, and barrel. We'll even name the city after the winner.
DEMETER:	And the city gets to keep both gifts. Right?
ZEUS:	Of course. Let's begin. You have one hour to shop and come up with a gift.
ATHENA:	Which way is the mall?
POSEIDON:	Outta my way! I've got places to go!
N1:	By the end of the hour, all the Olympians were gathered and waiting for the presentation of the gifts.
ZEUS:	We'll flip a coin to see who goes first.
POSEIDON:	Heads!
ATHENA:	Tails!
ZEUS:	*(flips coin)* Heads it is!
ARES:	Way to go, Poseidon!
POSEIDON:	*(stands while holding trident, swaggers forward)* Wait till you see this. You're gonna love it. *(raises trident high and thrusts it toward ground)*
D6:	Wow! Look at all that water coming up out of the ground!

ALL: Oooh! Aaah! *(DEITIES applaud)*

ZEUS: Nice trick, Poseidon. But what good is it?

POSEIDON: This is seawater, Chief. Get it? What is the most dangerous, the most unpredictable realm in the universe?

D7:   The sea!

POSEIDON: Of course. The city that controls the sea controls the world. That's my gift—control of the sea.

ARES: Might makes right, and right makes rich. Right?

POSEIDON: Right! Sea power! That's the name of the game.

ALL: Oooh! Aaah!

ZEUS: Well, Poseidon. This is a splendid gift.

D7:   Awesome!

ZEUS: But the contest isn't over, is it? We have another contestant.

N2:   Zeus was tempted to call the whole thing off and declare Poseidon the winner. It didn't seem likely that Athena could come up with anything to outshine Poseidon's gift.

N1:   It would be such a shame to embarrass Athena. After all, she was Zeus's very own daughter.

DEMETER: *(loud stage whisper)* Zeus! She'll never forgive you if you end the contest now. She's always been a headstrong girl. Go on and give her a chance.

ZEUS: *(to himself)* Oh well, what baaad could happen?
(to audience) Ladies and gentlemen! Contestant number two hails directly from the head of her daddy. She loves the spear and the shield. But she still finds time for her favorite hobby—weaving. And let us not forget that she was valedictorian of her graduating class at Mount Olympus High School. Let's hear a big round of applause for a very talented little lady—Athena!
(DEITIES applaud)

D2:   You go, girl!

ATHENA:	*(smiles, steps forward, holds up a small potted plant)* My gift to the city!
ALL:	Boo! Hiss! *(POSEIDON and ARES trade high-fives)*
ZEUS:	Athena! You better come up with an explanation mighty quick or you're gonna be the laughing stock of Mount Olympus.
ATHENA:	Why? What's wrong, Pop?
ZEUS:	What's wrong? We were supposed to have a real contest here. How do you expect to compete with a gift as grand as sea power when all you're giving is a…a…a potted plant!?
ARES:	Wussy gift, Athena babe! Now all the ladies in Poseidonia can have nice little potted plants to pretty up their houses. La-dee-dah!
ATHENA:	Oh, ye of little faith! This is no mere potted plant. *(to POSEIDON)* Watch and weep, pal! *(ATHENA pantomimes digging a hole; places pot in hole)*
N2:	And then, summoning all the power that only a goddess can muster, she caused the plant to grow to full maturity. *(ATHENA waves arms over plant)*
ATHENA:	Behold! The olive tree!
DEMETER:	Oooh, Aaah.
D2:	What's that all about?
D3:	Beats me.
D4:	I think she said it's an olive tree.
ATHENA:	Let me tell you about the olive. From the olive will come oil for cooking and for lighting homes. The olive will bring great wealth to this city. With that wealth, all the mortals here will live comfortable lives and will have time for learning, for music and theatre and philosophy. So you see, from this simple potted plant, the olive tree, this city—*my* city—will receive the greatest gift of all: *wisdom!*
ALL:	Oooh! Aaah! *(DEITIES applaud loudly)*

ZEUS: All right, everybody, calm down. We still have to vote.

N1:   All the male gods gathered around Poseidon and began to chant…

ALL (MALES):   Sea power! Sea power! Sea power!

N2:   Meanwhile, the goddesses gathered around Athena and began to chant…

ALL (FEMALES):   Wisdom! Wisdom! Wisdom!

N1:   So, who won?

N2:   Well, you may recall that there were twelve Olympians: six gods and six goddesses. But when the votes were cast, Zeus—as chairman of the board—abstained.

N1:   Athena won, six to five.

ZEUS: This new city will be called Athens—the city of Athena!

POSEIDON: But don't forget—with *my* gift, it will become the greatest sea power among all Greek cities.

ATHENA: And with my gift, it will become a prosperous city and a center of learning.

N2:   And that's the story of the naming of the magnificent city of Athens…

N1:   A city that learned to balance wealth with wisdom…

N2:   And power with peace.

ALL: Oooh! Aaah!

FOLKTALES

Aaron Kelly is Dead!

A Traditional Folktale

Scripted for Story Theatre by Barbara McBride-Smith

Cast of eight:
NARRATOR 1 (N1)   UNDERTAKER
NARRATOR 2 (N2)   FIDDLER
AARON KELLY   SOUND 1
WIDOW   SOUND 2

N1:   Aaron Kelly is dead!

ALL: Who cares?

UNDER: Good riddance!

N2:   That's right, Aaron Kelly was dead and nobody cared. He had been so mean and rotten when he was alive, nobody was sorry to see him go.

N1:   His widow got him a new suit and a coffin and put him in the ground.

N2:   She never even shed a tear for him.

WIDOW: Good-bye, Aaron Kelly! I'll not be seeing you again in this life.

N1:   But that night after the funeral, Aaron Kelly climbed out of his grave and walked home.

N2:   His widow was sitting by the fire, thinking how peaceful it was without old Aaron around, when he walked right in the door and said…

AARON: What's going on here? Why are you all dressed up in black? Who died?

WIDOW: You did! I buried you!

AARON: I ain't dead. I feel fine.

WIDOW: Well, you're not fine. You're dead. Get on back to that graveyard where you belong!

AARON: Look here, old woman, I'm not getting back in that coffin until I feel dead.

N1:	Aaron Kelly was still as mean and ornery as when he was alive.
N2:	He sat down in his favorite rocking chair, and he stayed there… rocking back and forth…back and forth.
SOUND 1:	Creak, creak…Creak, creak.
N1:	Days went by. Weeks went by. And Aaron Kelly just kept on rocking.
SOUND 1:	Creak, creak…Creak, creak.
N2:	After a month went by, Aaron Kelley began to dry up. His hair disappeared. His skin disappeared.
N1:	He was nothing but a skeleton. But he kept on rocking.
SOUND 1:	Creak, creak…Creak, creak.
N2:	And as he rocked, his bones clicked and clacked.
SOUND 2:	Click-clack. *(clack wooden sticks together, shake wooden wind chimes, or use a Vibra Slap)*
WIDOW:	Aaron Kelly, you're nothing but a pile of bones. Get on back to the graveyard where you belong.
AARON:	Not a chance. I still don't feel dead.
N1:	One evening the undertaker came to Widow Kelly's door.
UNDER:	Widow Kelly, I am so sorry to bother you, but there is a problem. You have not yet paid me for your husband's coffin.
WIDOW:	Indeed, sir, there *is* a problem. My husband won't stay in his coffin. He refuses to believe he is dead. He just sits here and rocks.
SOUND 1&2:	Creak, creak…Creak, creak. Click-clack…Click-clack.
UNDER:	Heavens! How can this be? We had a funeral. We put him in the ground.
WIDOW:	Until he *stays* in the ground, I can't collect his life insurance. And until I collect his life insurance, I can't pay you for that coffin.

Barbara McBride-Smith

UNDER:	I understand, Widow Kelly. What a pity.
N2:	Another month passed. The widow went about her chores, trying her best to ignore old Aaron Kelly. She kept hoping he would be reasonable and return to his coffin.
N1:	But that old skeleton called Aaron Kelly just kept sitting there... rocking and clacking.
SOUND 1&2:	Creak, creak...Creak, creak. Click-clack...Click-clack.
N2:	One night, the best fiddler in the county came to court Aaron Kelly's widow. She was pleased for his company. They sat down on the sofa to talk.
N1:	Old Aaron Kelly sat opposite them in his rocking chair. He was grinning and rocking and clacking.
SOUND 1&2:	Creak, creak...Creak, creak. Click-clack...Click-clack.
FIDDLER:	What's he doing here? Isn't he dead?
WIDOW:	Yes, of course he's dead. Just ignore him.
FIDDLER:	How long is he planning to stay?
WIDOW:	I don't know. Pretend he's not here.
FIDDLER:	But he's a skeleton. He should be in his coffin in the ground.
WIDOW:	*I* know that, and *you* know that, but *he* doesn't know that!
FIDDLER:	Can't you make him stop rattling his bones?
WIDOW:	Hmmm. I have an idea. Fiddler, play us a tune. I feel like dancing.
AARON:	Good idea! I feel like dancing, too!
N2:	So the fiddler took out his fiddle and began to play.
SOUND 1:	*(fiddle music begins, then fades and continues under following lines)*
N1:	Aaron Kelly heard that music, and he couldn't stay still. He jumped up, shook out his bones, and began to dance.
SOUND 2:	*(click-clack in time to fiddle music)*

N2:	Round and round he went, his toe bones tapping and his finger bones snapping.
N1:	His arm bones squeaking and his leg bones creaking.
WIDOW:	Play faster, fiddler!
AARON:	Yippee! Look at me! I'm a dancing fool!
N2:	All of a sudden, a bone broke loose from Aaron Kelly and flew through the air. It landed on the floor.
SOUND 2:	*(two wooden blocks hit together)*
FIDDLER:	Why, look at that! He's falling apart!
WIDOW:	Keep playing, fiddler! Faster!
SOUND 1:	*(music speeds up)*
N2:	The fiddler played faster, and another one of Aaron Kelly's bones came flying off and hit the floor.
SOUND 2:	*(two wooden blocks hit together)*
WIDOW:	Play louder, fiddler!
SOUND 1:	*(music gets louder)*
N1:	The fiddler played that fiddle so loud and so hard, he could barely hang on to it. Aaron Kelly's bones were flying and dropping all over the place.
SOUND 1&2:	*(music gets louder and wooden sticks hit together)*
N1:	Soon nothing was left of him but a pile of disconnected bones…and his old bald skeleton head.
SOUND 1:	*(fiddle music fades out)*
N2:	That head looked up at the fiddler, snapped its yellow teeth, and hollered…
AARON:	By cracky, ain't we having fun now?!
FIDDLER:	I give up. Good-bye, Widow Kelly.

WIDOW:	*(sadly)* Good-bye, fiddler. *(angrily)* And good-bye to you too, Aaron Kelly. I'm taking you back to the graveyard where you belong.
AARON:	Oh, nooooooo!
N1:	The widow gathered up Aaron Kelly's bones and carried them to the graveyard. She mixed them up real good before she put them in his coffin. And old Aaron Kelly never did pull himself together again.
N2:	And Widow Kelly never did get married again either, which suited her just fine. She collected Aaron Kelly's life insurance, paid her debts, and went dancing every chance she got. And you can be *dead sure* she lived happily...
WIDOW:	And peacefully...
N2:	Ever after.
SOUND 2:	*(two wooden blocks hit together twice)*

Finn M'Coul

An Irish Folktale

Scripted for Story Theatre by Barbara McBride-Smith

Cast of nine:
NARRATOR 1 (N1)   MESSENGER
NARRATOR 2 (N2)   GRANIA
NARRATOR 3 (N3)   CUCULLIN
FINN   SOUND
OONAGH

N1:   There once was a giant named Finn M'Coul. He was the biggest and bravest giant in all of Ireland. His great deeds were known far and wide.

N2:   And Finn M'Coul was so gentle, wild animals lay down before him.

N3:   There was also a giant named Cucullin who lived in Ireland. He was almost as big as Finn M'Coul. But this giant was so fierce that wild animals ran away from him.

N2:   He was always looking for a fight. Every giant in Ireland had been given a good beating by Cucullin.

N3:   Every giant, that is, except Finn M'Coul.

N1:   Cucullin had once caught a thunderbolt and flattened it. He carried it around in his pocket to show how strong he was.

N2:   But the true secret of his strength lay in his brass finger on his right hand.

N3:   One summer day, Finn M'Coul was away from home building a bridge with his kinfolk when he saw a messenger galloping toward him.

MESSENGER: Finn! Finn M'Coul! I have bad news for you!

FINN: Tell me, man! My good wife Oonagh hasn't taken sick, has she?

MESSENGER: No, Finn. The lovely Oonagh is fine. But she sent me to tell you that Cucullin is headed right for your house on Knockmany Hill. He's looking to fight with you.

FINN:	So, he's coming, is he? Then I'll not disappoint him.
N1:	Finn ran as fast as his giant legs could carry him. He went up Knockmany Hill the back way.
N2:	He found his wife waiting for him.
FINN:	Oonagh, is it true? Cucullin is coming to fight me? Is he as big and fierce as they say?
OONAGH:	He's coming, all right. Can you feel the ground shaking? As for how he looks, I'll ask my sister Grania. She lives on the next hill across the valley.
N3:	Oonagh stepped outside and called across the valley to her sister.
OONAGH:	Grania! Are you home? Look this way—to the bottom of Knockmany Hill. Tell me what you see.
GRANIA:	Yes, I'm outside in my vegetable garden. I'm looking now. Oh dear me! What I see is the most terrible giant I've ever seen. He's almost as big as Finn, but he's an angry fellow. His eyes are rolling around like the hands on a clock. Steam is coming out the top of his head. The birds are falling out of the trees in fright.
OONAGH:	My dear sister, please do me a favor. Call down to that giant. His name is Cucullin. Invite him to your house for a bite to eat. Delay him as long as you can.
GRANIA:	I'd be glad to help you, Oonagh. But I don't have a thing in the house to satisfy the hunger of such a giant. He doesn't look like the vegetable salad sort of fellow.
OONAGH:	I'll fling you some bacon and butter and bread across. Catch! Be sure to keep him there a goodly amount of time.
GRANIA:	I'll do my best. Will Finn be getting ready to fight or will he be running away?
FINN:	I've never cared much for fighting. This monster could be dangerous. Perhaps running is a good idea.
OONAGH:	Now, Finn. It's time you stopped avoiding that bully Cucullin. Let's settle things with him once and for all.

FINN:	I could try to reason with him. But he won't listen. He'll flatten me to a pancake just like that thunderbolt he carries in his pocket. My courage is leaving me. I'd better run.
OONAGH:	No, Finn, stay right here. You have *me* to help you. Two heads are better than one.
GRANIA:	Yoo-hoo! Mr. Cucullin! I see you down there! Won't you come up and join me for a bit of lunch?
N1:	While Grania delayed that bully Cucullin, Oonagh began to work a charm the fairies had taught her. She took nine woolen threads, each a different color. She braided them into three braids.
N2:	She put one around her right arm, one around her right ankle, and the third she hung over her heart.
N3:	Now Oonagh was protected, and she could think clearly about what she should do.
OONAGH:	Finn, go up to the attic and gather as many iron frying pans as you can find. Fetch them down to me while I'm mixing some bread.
N1:	Oonagh took the dozen iron pans that Finn brought her and baked them inside a dozen loaves of bread.
OONAGH:	Now, I'll just put these loaves in the cupboard with the bread I baked yesterday.
N2:	Then she took a pot of milk and made it into cheese. She shaped the white cheese into smooth, round chunks, and she placed them in a bowl along with some round white rocks.
FINN:	Is there anything else I can do, my dear Oonagh?
OONAGH:	As a matter of fact, Finn, there is. You can build a baby cradle with this stack of wood.
N3:	When Finn was done with making the cradle, she handed him some very large baby clothes she had sewn.
OONAGH:	Put on these baby clothes and hop into the cradle, Finn. When Cucullin gets here, try to look sweet and innocent.

SOUND:	Knock-knock!
FINN:	There's Cucullin at the door now. May luck be with us!
CUCULLIN:	All right, woman! Open the door! Where's that coward Finn M'Coul?
OONAGH:	Good evening to you, Mr. Cucullin. My husband Finn is off working on a bridge with his kinfolk, but I'm expecting him home this very evening. Won't you come in and wait for him?
N1:	Cucullin stepped into the house. He pulled the flattened thunderbolt from his pocket.
CUCULLIN:	See this? This *was* a thunderbolt. I flattened it. And that's exactly what I'm going to do to Finn M'Coul when he gets here. Heh, heh, heh…
OONAGH:	Well, that may not be as easy as you think. My husband Finn is a hulk of a man. Just take a look at our little baby here in this cradle and you'll get a bit of an idea of the size and strength of Finn himself.
N2:	Cucullin peeked in the cradle, and Finn peeked back at him.
FINN:	Goo!
CUCULLIN:	'Tis a mighty big lad you've got there. He must eat well.
OONAGH:	Oh yes, indeed. Speaking of eating, we were just about to have our supper. Will you join us?
N3:	Since Cucullin was always hungry, he couldn't resist. Oonagh took one of the loaves of bread from the cupboard and handed it to him.
CUCULLIN:	Yum-yum.
SOUND:	Clang! Clang!
CUCULLIN:	Yow! What's in this bread? Two of my teeth just fell out!
OONAGH:	That's Finn's favorite bread. Is it a wee bit too tough for you?
CUCULLIN:	Too tough for me? I should say not. Give me another loaf!
OONAGH:	Here you go. My own special recipe, it is.

Barbara McBride-Smith

N1:	Cucullin bit into that loaf, which also had an iron pan inside it...
SOUND:	Clang! Clang!
CUCULLIN:	Yow! I just lost another couple of teeth. I'm getting angry, woman!
FINN:	Waaa! Waaa! Hungry, hungry, hungry!
OONAGH:	Oh, my sweet dumplin'. Would you like some bread?
FINN:	Goo!
OONAGH:	Here you go, a loaf for you.
FINN:	Yum-yum. *(gobbles bread)* More, more.
N2:	The baby gobbled down three more loaves of bread, which, of course, had no iron pans inside them. Cucullin began to worry. He thought to himself...
CUCULLIN:	If this is the son, then how strong must the father be?
N3:	But he said to Oonagh...
CUCULLIN:	I see that Finn M'Coul's son is a very healthy lad.
OONAGH:	Aye, and a lot like his daddy he is. Instead of toys, he loves to play with stones. See these nice white ones here? Here you go, my sweet little lamb. Show the man what you can do.
N1:	Finn grabbed hold of that stone...
N2:	...which was really a cheese...
N1:	...and he squeezed it until all the water ran out of it. Then he popped it into his mouth and swallowed it.
FINN:	Yum-yum.
CUCULLIN:	Here. Give me one of those stones. I won't be outdone by a baby.
N2:	Cucullin grabbed a real stone and squeezed. He squeezed and squeezed. But no matter how hard he squeezed, he couldn't get one drop out of that stone.

N1:   So, he popped the stone into his mouth and chomped down on it…

SOUND: Clang! Clang! Clang!

CUCULLIN: Yow-ow-ow! There go the rest of my teeth! Thunderin' lizards! I'm really losing my temper now. How can that baby eat rocks? What kind of teeth does he have? All right, little dumplin', let me see your choppers.

N3:   Baby Finn opened his mouth wide, and Cucullin stuck in his brass finger—the very same brass finger that was the secret of his strength.

SOUND: Crunch!

FINN: Yum-yum.

CUCULLIN: Yow-ow-ow-ow! My brass finger! My strength! They're gone!

FINN: And now here I come—Finn M'Coul himself—to pound the living daylights out of you, Cucullin!

CUCULLIN: Please, I beg of you, Finn M'Coul. Let me go in peace. I'll tell everyone what a great and honorable hero you are. I'll go home, and I'll never set foot on Knockmany Hill again.

OONAGH: Are you telling the truth, Mr. Cucullin?

CUCULLIN: Yes, yes. Finn M'Coul is the greatest giant in the world.

OONAGH: Aye, that he is. And a good and fair man, too. Why not let him go, Finn? He'll not bother you again.

FINN: Hmmm, so be it. I never really cared much for fighting anyway. Good-bye, Cucullin!

N1:   So, out the door went Cucullin.

N2:   He never picked a fight with anyone…ever again.

N3:   And Finn M'Coul and his clever wife Oonagh lived a long and happy life.

Barbara McBride-Smith

Sody Salleratus

An Appalachian Folktale

Scripted for Story Theatre by Barbara McBride-Smith

Cast of eight, plus any number of choral speakers in CHORUS:

NARRATOR	OLD MAN
LITTLE BOY	GROCER
LITTLE GIRL	BEAR
OLD WOMAN	SQUIRREL

NARRATOR: Once upon a time in an old house in the woods, there lived…

OLD WOMAN: An old woman…

OLD MAN: And an old man…

LITTLE BOY: And a little boy…

LITTLE GIRL: And a little girl…

SQUIRREL: And a squirrel.

NARRATOR: One day the old woman wanted to bake some biscuits, but she didn't have any baking soda.

OLD WOMAN: Little boy, go into town and buy me some Sody Salleratus. And don't be dilly-dallying along the way. You hurry right back.

LITTLE BOY: Yes, ma'am. I'll hurry right back.

CHORUS: Sody, Sody, Sody Salleratus.

NARRATOR: The little boy went a-skippin' down the road.

CHORUS: Sody, Sody, Sody Salleratus.

NARRATOR: He went over the bridge.

CHORUS: Sody, Sody, Sody Salleratus.

NARRATOR: He walked right into the store.

LITTLE BOY: Hey, Mr. Grocer! May I have some Sody Salleratus, please?

GROCER: Sody Salleratus? Oh, you want some baking soda. All right. Here you go. *(hands big orange baking soda box to boy)*

LITTLE BOY:	Thanks, Mr. Grocer. Here's a nickel.
GROCER:	Now, don't be dilly-dallying on the way home.
LITTLE BOY:	No, sir. I won't do any dilly-dallying.
NARRATOR:	The little boy headed back down the road toward home.
CHORUS:	Sody, Sody, Sody Salleratus.
NARRATOR:	He went across the bridge.
CHORUS:	Sody, Sody, Sody Salleratus.
NARRATOR:	Now, under that bridge there lived a big, ol', ugly, hairy, mean bear. He was sound asleep, but he woke up.
BEAR:	*Grrr!* Who's that walking on my bridge?
LITTLE BOY:	It's me. A little boy. Me and my Sody Salleratus.
BEAR:	*Rawrrr!* I'm gonna eat you up. You and your Sody Salleratus! *Gulp!*
NARRATOR:	And he did. Meanwhile, back at the house, the old woman and the old man and the little girl and the squirrel waited and waited for the little boy to come back. Finally, the old woman said…
OLD WOMAN:	Little girl, go down the road and see if you can find that little boy. Him and my Sody Salleratus. And don't be dilly-dallying along the way
LITTLE GIRL:	Yes, ma'am. I won't do any dilly-dallying. I'll hurry right back.
NARRATOR:	So, off she went a-skippin' down the road.
CHORUS:	Sody, Sody, Sody Salleratus.
NARRATOR:	She went over that bridge.
CHORUS:	Sody, Sody, Sody Salleratus.
BEAR:	*Grrr!* Who's that walking on my bridge?
GIRL:	It's me. A little girl.
BEAR:	*Rawrrr!* I ate a little boy. Him and his Sody Salleratus. And now I'm gonna eat you, too! *Gulp!*

Barbara McBride-Smith

NARRATOR:	And he did. Meanwhile, back at the house, the old woman and the old man and the squirrel waited and waited for the little boy and the little girl to come back. Finally, the old woman said…
OLD WOMAN:	Old man, go down that road and see if you can find that little girl and that little boy and my Sody Salleratus. And don't be dilly-dallying along the way.
OLD MAN:	Yes, ma'am. I won't do any dilly-dallying. I'll hurry right back.
NARRATOR:	So, the old man went a-hobblin' down the road.
CHORUS:	Sody, Sody, Sody Salleratus.
NARRATOR:	He went across that bridge.
CHORUS:	Sody, Sody, Sody Salleratus.
BEAR:	*Grrr!* Who's that walking on my bridge?
OLD MAN:	It's me. An old man.
BEAR:	*Rawrrr!* I ate a little girl. I ate a little boy. Him and his Sody Salleratus. And now I'm gonna eat you, too! *Gulp!*
NARRATOR:	And he did. Meanwhile, back at the house, the old woman and the squirrel waited and waited for the old man and the little girl and the little boy to come back. Finally, the old woman said…
OLD WOMAN:	Well, if you want anything done right, you gotta do it yourself! I'll go find that old man and that little girl and that little boy, *and* my Sody Salleratus.
NARRATOR:	So, that old woman went a-limpin' down the road.
CHORUS:	Sody, Sody, Sody Salleratus.
NARRATOR:	She went over that bridge.
CHORUS:	Sody, Sody, Sody Salleratus.
BEAR:	*Grrr!* Who's that walking on my bridge?
OLD WOMAN:	It's me. An old woman.
BEAR:	*Rawrrr!* I ate an old man. I ate a little girl. I ate a little boy. Him and his Sody Salleratus. And now I'm gonna eat you, too! *Gulp!*

NARRATOR: And he did. Meanwhile, back at the house, the squirrel waited and waited for the old woman and the old man and the little girl and the little boy to come back.

SQUIRREL: I'm hungry! If I'm ever gonna get any biscuits, I'd better go find that old woman and that old man and that little girl and that little boy. *And* that Sody Salleratus.

NARRATOR: The squirrel went a-hoppin' down the road.

CHORUS: Sody, Sody, Sody Salleratus.

NARRATOR: He went over the bridge.

CHORUS: Sody, Sody, Sody Salleratus.

BEAR: *Grrr!* Who's that walking on my bridge?

SQUIRREL: It's me. A squirrel.

BEAR: *Rawrrr!* Well, I ate an old woman. I ate an old man. I ate a little girl. I ate a little boy. Him and his Sody Salleratus. I might as well eat you, too!

SQUIRREL: You gotta catch me first!

NARRATOR: The squirrel ran to a tree and climbed up and up and up.
(SQUIRREL pantomimes climbing)
The bear ran to the tree and climbed up and up and up.
(BEAR pantomimes climbing)

SQUIRREL: I'm going higher!

BEAR: I'm going higher, too!

SQUIRREL: I'm gonna run out on this branch!

BEAR: I'm gonna run out on this branch, too!

SQUIRREL: I'm gonna jump up and down on this branch!

CHORUS: Boing. Boing. Boing. *(SQUIRREL pantomimes jumping)*

NARRATOR: The squirrel took a flying leap and landed in another tree.

BEAR: I'm gonna jump up and down on this branch, too!
(BEAR pantomimes jumping)

Barbara McBride-Smith

CHORUS: Bonk...Bonk...*Crack!*

NARRATOR: The branch broke.

BEAR: *Rawrrr!* I'm falling! Helllp!

NARRATOR: Down, down, down fell the bear.

CHORUS: *Ka-Boom!* (BEAR *falls to floor and stretches out*)

NARRATOR: The bear busted wide open. And out of his belly stepped the old woman and the old man and the little girl and the little boy.

OLD WOMAN: Little boy, where's my Sody Salleratus?

LITTLE BOY: Right here, ma'am!

OLD WOMAN: Good. Let's go home.

NARRATOR: So, they all went down the road toward the little house.

CHORUS: Sody, Sody, Sody Salleratus.

NARRATOR: That night the old woman baked a big heap of biscuits with that Sody Salleratus. Everybody ate and ate and ate.

OLD MAN,
LITTLE GIRL,
LITTLE BOY: (*rubbing their tummies*) Yum-yum, good!

NARRATOR: And guess who ate the most biscuits of all?

SQUIRREL: (*rubbing his tummy*) Yum-yum, good!

NARRATOR: And after they were full, they lived happily ever after.

CHORUS: Sody, Sody, Sody Salleratus.

(BEAR *holds up sign that says* "THE END")

The Squire's Bride

A Norwegian Folktale

Scripted for Story Theatre by Barbara McBride-Smith

Cast of six:
NARRATOR 1 (N1)	GIRL
NARRATOR 2 (N2)	FARMER
SQUIRE	LAD

N1: There was once a very wealthy squire. He owned a lot of land and a big house. And he had plenty of money in the bank.

N2: What the squire did not have was a wife.

N1: One day the squire was walking through his hayfield. He saw a girl hard at work.

N2: The girl's father was a poor farmer, and the squire decided that this girl would be lucky to marry a rich man such as himself.

SQUIRE: Hello, my dear girl. I've been thinking of getting married.

GIRL: That's nice.

SQUIRE: You would be a good wife for me.

GIRL: Thank you, sir. But I don't think I'd like to be your wife.

SQUIRE: Of course you would! I have acres of land and a big house and a lot of money.

GIRL: I'm really not interested in those things, sir.

SQUIRE: You're lucky I've chosen you. Go on. Say you'll marry me.

GIRL: No, I really don't want to marry you.

SQUIRE: But I insist!

GIRL: Go away!

N1: The squire was not accustomed to being refused. He decided he might have better luck if he talked to the girl's father.

SQUIRE: I say there, good farmer. Do you remember that money you owe me?

FARMER:	Yes.
SQUIRE:	And do you remember that nice piece of land right next to your farm that you'd like to own?
FARMER:	Yes.
SQUIRE:	Well, you don't owe me the money any more.
FARMER:	Yes?
SQUIRE:	And that nice piece of land is yours.
FARMER:	Yes?
SQUIRE:	*If* you convince your daughter to marry me!
FARMER:	It's a deal. Leave everything to me.
N2:	That evening, the farmer tried to talk his daughter into marrying the squire.
FARMER:	My sweet daughter, I've been thinking. It's time you got married.
GIRL:	No, Father. I don't want to get married.
FARMER:	But the squire is willing to take you as his bride.
GIRL:	He's not my type.
FARMER:	He's very rich.
GIRL:	He's a miser! I won't marry him.
FARMER:	I give up.
N1:	The squire waited and waited for his bride. When she didn't arrive, he got angry. He sent for the girl's father.
SQUIRE:	You promised me your daughter. Now you must keep your promise!
FARMER:	But, sir, my daughter has a mind of her own. She's…uh, not ready to get married yet.
SQUIRE:	You want that nice piece of land, don't you? You want to be rid of your debt, don't you?

Barbara McBride-Smith

FARMER:	I see what you mean. Hmmmm, let me think… *(pantomimes thinking hard)* There's only one thing left to do.
SQUIRE:	Yes, tell me.
FARMER:	Get everything ready for the wedding. Invite all the guests. Be sure the preacher is ready and waiting. Then send for my daughter. She'll think you want her to do some work. But as soon as she gets to your house, marry her! Don't give her a chance to say no.
SQUIRE:	What a marvelous idea! Ha! She'll be my wife before she knows it!
N2:	So, the next day everyone at the squire's house got ready.
N1:	They cooked the wedding feast.
N2:	They baked the wedding cake.
N1:	They sewed the wedding dress.
N2:	They cut the wedding flowers.
N1:	They invited the wedding guests.
N2:	And then, they sent for the preacher.
N1:	Everything was ready. It was time to get the bride.
N2:	The squire shouted to one of his farm lads…
SQUIRE:	Run down to the farmer's house and tell him to send me what he has promised. And be quick about it!
N1:	The lad ran as fast as he could to the farmer's house.
LAD:	Sir, my master wants me to bring whatever you have promised him. And please hurry!
FARMER:	Oh yes. She's out in the meadow. Just run out there and take her.
N2:	When the lad reached the meadow, he found the daughter raking hay.
LAD:	Good morning, Miss. I've come to fetch whatever it is your father promised my master.

N1:	Now, the girl was very clever, and she guessed what her father and the squire were up to.
GIRL:	Yes, of course. My father promised a donkey to your master. It's that little gray one grazing over there. You go right ahead and take her. Your master will be pleased to see her.
N2:	The boy jumped on the donkey's back and rode her to the squire's house as fast as he could. He tied her to the fence and ran into the house.
SQUIRE:	Aha! You're back! Did you bring her with you?
LAD:	Yes, sir. She's just outside…
SQUIRE:	Good. Now take her upstairs.
LAD:	Upstairs, master?
SQUIRE:	Yes, what's the matter with you? Upstairs and into the dressing room.
LAD:	But, I'm not sure I can get her to go up those stairs.
SQUIRE:	Well, if *you* can't persuade her, then get someone to help you. And hurry!
N1:	The boy knew he must not argue. So he gathered up all the farm hands to help him. Some of them pulled at the donkey's head, and some of them pushed at her behind. Finally, they got her up the stairs.
LAD:	Whew! It's done, master. She is upstairs and in the dressing room. But, sir, that was the hardest job I've ever had to do.
SQUIRE:	What a complainer. Surely it wasn't that difficult. She's really very fond of me, you know.
LAD:	*(to himself)* What's wrong with him today?
SQUIRE:	Now, send the women up to dress her. Tell them that the wedding gown and the veil are waiting in the closet. And tell them not to forget her flowers.
LAD:	A wedding gown, sir…and flowers…for a…a…
SQUIRE:	Yes, for a wedding! Now be quick about it.

Barbara McBride-Smith

N2:	The lad ran into the kitchen and told the women what they were supposed to do.
LAD:	Our master is playing a little joke on his guests today. You are to go upstairs and dress a donkey as a bride.
N1:	The women laughed at first. But then they ran upstairs and dressed the donkey in all the wedding finery. And they didn't forget the flowers.
LAD:	She is ready, master.
SQUIRE:	Good. Bring her down. I am certain she will be delighted to see me. My guests and the preacher are waiting.
LAD:	Yes, master. Whatever you say.
N2:	There was a loud clatter and thumping and bumping on the stairs as the donkey was led down. The door was thrown open to the large room where the squire and all his guests were waiting.
N1:	And it was then that the squire saw the little gray donkey in the wedding dress.
SQUIRE:	Aaarrrrrggghhh!! No! No! No!
N2:	The guests looked at the squire…and then at the donkey.
N1:	And they all burst out laughing.
ALL:	(CAST laughs)
N1:	The squire did not get married that day…
N2:	Or any other day.

The Wolf and the Seven Kids
A Folktale from the Brothers Grimm

Scripted for Story Theatre by Barbara McBride-Smith

Cast of twelve: NARRATOR 1 (N1)   WOLF
                  NARRATOR 2 (N2)   KIDS 1, 2, 3, 4, 5, 6, 7
                  NANNY GOAT   SOUND

N1: Once there was a Nanny Goat who had seven little kids. Those kids were as good as good can be, and their mama loved them very much.

N2: One day the Nanny Goat said to her children…

NANNY: I must go to the market today, children. I won't be home until late. While I'm gone, be watchful and be wary. I've heard tell that the big, bad Wolf has been seen hanging around these woods.

KID 2: Ooooo!

NANNY: Whatever you do, don't let the big, bad Wolf into the house. Because if the big, bad Wolf gets into the house, he will eat you up.

KIDS 3&4: Ooooo!

KID 1: Never fear, Mother dear. We will never, never, never let the big, bad Wolf into the house.

KIDS 5&6: Never, never, never.

N1: So, the Nanny Goat slipped her shopping basket over her arm and went out the door and down the path.

KID 7: Hurry! Let's shut the door and lock it tight.

N2: As soon as the Nanny Goat was out of sight, who do you think appeared?

WOLF: Hello! It's me—the big, bad Wolf!

N2: Yes. It was the big, bad Wolf.

N1: He ran up to the little house and knocked on the door.

SOUND: Blam! Blam!

KID 2: Who's there?

WOLF: *(in a deep gruff voice)* It is I—your mother! Open up the door and let me in!

KID 3: *(to other kids)* But our mother said she wouldn't be home until late.

KID 4: Is it late yet?

KID 5: Maybe our mother came home early.

KID 6: Could it be our mother at the door?

WOLF: Hurry up and open the door!

KID 1: Wait just a minute. Our mother has a soft, sweet voice. And whoever is at the door has a gruff, harsh voice.

KID 7: *(to WOLF)* You're not our mother! You're the big, bad Wolf. And we won't let you in!

WOLF: Arrrgh! Curses! I thought I fooled 'em.

N2: So the big, bad Wolf ran all the way through the woods and into town.

N1: He slipped into the back storage room of a store and stole a box of chalk.

WOLF: Heh, heh, heh. I told ya I was the big, bad Wolf.

N2: The Wolf chewed up a piece of that chalk and swallowed it.

WOLF: Gulp! Yech!

N1: Believe it or not, this made the Wolf's voice all soft and sweet.

N2: The Wolf ran all the way back through the woods and knocked on the door of the little house.

SOUND: Blam! Blam!

KID 2: Who's there?

WOLF:	*(in fake soft, sweet voice)* It is I, your mother. Open up the door, children, and let me in.
KID 3:	But our mother said she wouldn't be home until late.
KID 4:	Is it late now?
KID 5:	Maybe it's late enough.
KID 6:	Whoever is at the door has a soft, sweet voice.
KID 7:	Wait a minute. I've got an idea. *(whispers something to KID 1)*
KID 1:	Come to the window and show us your feet!
WOLF:	*(slightly angry sweet voice)* Not now, children. Mommy's feet are tired.
KIDS 1&7:	Come to the window and show us your feet!
WOLF:	Very well. If you insist, children.
N1:	The Wolf ran to the window, lay down on the ground…
N2:	…and threw his big feet into the air.
KIDS 2&3:	Uh-oh!
KID 4:	Our mother has pretty, little, soft, white feet.
KID 5:	And you have horrible, hairy, dirty old feet!
KID 6:	You're not our mother!
KID 7:	You're the big, bad Wolf, and we won't let you in!
WOLF:	*(deep gruff voice has returned)* Arrrgh! Curses! Foiled again!
N1:	The Wolf ran all the way through the woods and back into town.
N2:	He slipped into the back of a bakery, found a barrel of flour…
N1:	…and dipped his back legs into the flour.
WOLF:	Heh, heh, heh. Look at my pretty, soft, white feet.
N2:	Then the Wolf took another piece of chalk from his pocket.
N1:	He chewed the chalk and swallowed it.

WOLF: Gulp! Yech!

N2:   Now the Wolf's voice was all soft and sweet again.

N1:   Balancing on his front legs, and holding his back legs in the air…

N2:   So they would stay clean and white…

N1:   The Wolf ran all the way through the woods, back to the little house, and knocked on the door.

SOUND: Blam! Blam!

KID 2:   Who's there?

WOLF: *(in fake soft, sweet voice)* It is I, your mother. Open up the door and let me in, children.

KID 3:   Our mother said she wouldn't be home until late.

KID 4:   Is it late now?

WOLF: *(angrily, but still in a sweet voice)* Yes! It's late already! Now, let me in!

KID 5:   Maybe it really is our mother.

KID 6:   Whoever is at the door has a soft, sweet voice.

KIDS 1&7:   Come to the window and show us your feet!

WOLF: Of course, children. Heh, heh, heh.

N2:   The Wolf ran over to the window, lay down on the ground, and threw those big back feet into the air.

KID 2:   Whoever was at the door *did* have a soft, sweet voice.

KID 3:   And whoever is at the window *does* have soft, white feet.

KID 7:   Did our mother's feet grow bigger during her long walk to the market?

KID 4:   Could it be our mother?

KID 5:   Yes! She's come home from the market.

KID 6:   Mother dear, come in, come in!

Barbara McBride-Smith

N1:	The seven little kids unlocked the door…
N2:	…threw it wide open…
WOLF:	*(gruff voice has returned)* Rawrrr! Fooled ya!
KIDS:	*(all shouting spontaneously)* Help! Help! Help!
N1:	The big, bad Wolf ran in and began to chase those seven little kids all over the house.
N2:	One by one, he caught them…
WOLF:	Got'cha! Got'cha! Got you, too!
N1:	And ate them.
WOLF:	Gulp! Gulp!
N2:	He swallowed those kids—except for the littlest one—who hid inside a grandfather clock.
WOLF:	Yum-yum. Let's see, now. How many was that? Oh, never mind. I must've got 'em all. There's not a kid in sight!
N1:	The Wolf was stuffed full. All he wanted to do was go home and sleep off his huge lunch.
N2:	So the Wolf dragged his big belly out the door and through the woods toward his den.
WOLF:	*(panting hard)* Ohhh, I am really tired. Maybe I should stop halfway and take a rest. This looks like a perfect place. A big shady tree, a sparkling stream. Ahhh yes, time for a nap.
N1:	The wolf stretched out under the tree and fell fast asleep.
WOLF:	*(snoring)* Zzzzzzz.
N2:	Meanwhile, back at the little house…
N1:	The Nanny Goat came home from the market.
NANNY:	Hello, children! I'm home!
N1:	But there was no answer.
NANNY:	Children? Yoo-hoo, where are you? *(pauses to listen)* Oh, dear.

SOUND:	Bong! Bong! Bong! *(sound of clock striking)*
N2:	And then the littlest kid opened the grandfather clock.
SOUND:	Creeeeak.
KID 7:	Oh, Mother dear. A terrible thing has happened! The big, bad Wolf came to our door. He made his voice all soft and sweet, and he made his feet all soft and white, and we thought he was you. And we opened up the door, and he ran into our house, and now he has eaten us all up—except for me. Whatever shall we do?
NANNY:	I know a thing or two about big, bad wolves. They're not half as smart as mother goats. Stop crying, little one, and come with me.
N1:	The Nanny Goat took the littlest kid's hoof in hers, and they began to walk through the woods.
N2:	Before long, they came upon that big, bad Wolf sleeping under the shady oak tree.
WOLF:	*(snoring)* Zzzzzzz.
N1:	His huge belly was spread out all around him.
N2:	His belly seemed to be jumping and kicking his insides.
SOUND:	Boing! Boing! Boing! Boing! *(use Vibra Slap to make bouncing sound)*
NANNY:	Hmmm. Just as I thought.
N1:	The Nanny Goat reached into her pocket and took out her sewing scissors. The kind with the sharp points.
N2:	She began to clip a hole in the Wolf's belly.
SOUND:	Snip-snip, snip-snip.
N1:	As soon as the hole was big enough, out jumped one of her little kids.
KID 6:	Mama!
N2:	She clipped the hole bigger.

Barbara McBride-Smith

SOUND:	Snip-snip, snip-snip.
N1:	And out jumped another little kid.
KID 5:	Mama!
N2:	She kept on clipping that hole bigger.
SOUND:	Snip-snip, snip-snip.
N1:	And one by one, her children jumped out of the Wolf's belly.
KID 4:	Mama!
KID 3:	Mama!
KID 2:	Mama!
KID 1:	Mama!
NANNY:	Oh, my darling little kids. Thank goodness you're alive and well.
N2:	You see, the big, bad Wolf had been so greedy, he had forgotten to chew. He had swallowed those little kids whole.
NANNY:	Now you must help me, children. Go quickly and find stones as big as yourselves. Bring them to me. Hurry, before the Wolf wakes up.
N1:	The little kids did as their mother said. They ran and found stones as big as themselves and brought them to the Nanny Goat.
N2:	She placed the stones inside the Wolf's belly.
NANNY:	And now for the finishing touch.
N1:	The Nanny Goat reached inside her other pocket and took out her sewing needle. The one with the very sharp point.
N2:	The Nanny Goat began to stitch the Wolf's belly closed.
NANNY:	*(humming softly—tune to " Rock-A-Bye Baby")* There! Such a fine seam. He'll never even know he's been cut open.
N1:	Then the Nanny Goat and her children ran quietly through the woods back to their little house.
N2:	Soon thereafter, the big, bad Wolf woke up.

WOLF: *(yawns)* Ohhh, my aching belly. I feel terrible. I feel miserable. I feel worse than the time I ate those foolish little pigs. I need some relief. *(searches in pockets)* Arrrgh! No Rolaids, no Alka Seltzer. What am I gonna do?

N1: And then the Wolf saw the sparkling stream of water nearby.

WOLF: Maybe a drink of water would help.

N2: The Wolf began to drag his body toward the stream.

WOLF: Curses! I feel as if I've eaten a bunch of rocks instead of a bunch of goats.

N1: The Wolf leaned over the stream to take a sip…

N2: …and suddenly, those heavy rocks in his belly shifted forward.

WOLF: Uh oh!

N1: The Wolf fell headfirst into the sparkling stream of water.

SOUND: Ker-splash!

N2: Those rocks inside him were so heavy, the Wolf went all the way to the bottom of the stream.

WOLF: Anchors aweigh! *Glub glub glub.*

N1: He must have liked it down there.

N2: Because he never came back up.

N1: And as for the Nanny Goat and her seven little kids…

NANNY: We'll never have to worry about the big, bad Wolf again.

ALL KIDS: *(clapping and cheering)* Yay!!!!

N2: And they lived happily ever after.

Barbara McBride-Smith

The Miller and His Donkey

An Aesop Fable

Scripted for Story Theatre by Barbara McBride-Smith

Cast of ten:

NARRATOR 1 (N1)	FARMER
NARRATOR 2 (N2)	GRANDMA 1
MILLER	GRANDMA 2
SON	JUDGE
DONKEY	LAWYER

N1: Once there was a miller who owned a very old donkey.

DONKEY: I am sooo old. Hee-haw!

N2: One sunny day the miller decided to take the old donkey to market and sell him.

MILLER: Get out of bed, Son, and get dressed. We're taking the donkey to the market today. A little money is worth more than an old donkey.

N1: So, the miller and his son started down the road leading the donkey with a rope.

SON: Father, it's a long way to the market. Can we ride the donkey?

MILLER: No, Son, not today. It's so hot he'd be all worn out by the time we rode into town. We want him to look good so we'll get more money for him.

DONKEY: Hee-haw. It sure is hot out here today.

N2: The three of them walked on down the road, and soon they met a farmer.

FARMER: How silly you are. Why are you walking when you have a donkey to ride?

MILLER: Silly? We're not silly! Climb up on that donkey, Son.

DONKEY: Hee-haw. That's a *big* boy. What a pain in the back.

N1: They went on down the road with the boy riding the old donkey.

N2: Before long, they met a peddler pushing his cart.

PEDDLER: What's this I see? A strong young boy riding while his old daddy walks? Aren't you ashamed, boy?

BOY: Uhhh, yes sir, I guess I am. Here, Father. I'll get down. You get up here and ride the donkey.

N1: The miller really wasn't tired at all, but he agreed.

MILLER: Good idea, Son. *I'll* ride the donkey and *you* walk.

N2: And so, they traded places.

DONKEY: Oh, good grief! This fella weighs twice as much as the boy. My poor aching back. Hee-haw.

N1: They went on down the road. And soon they met two old grandmas coming home from the market.

GRANDMA 1: Well, would you look at this! What a lazy daddy you are— riding along in comfort while your poor little boy has to walk.

GRANDMA 2: Tsk, tsk, tsk. You ought to be ashamed of yourself. A good parent always thinks of his child first.

MILLER: Oh, dear. I'm really confused now. All right, Son, get up here behind me. We'll both ride the donkey.

DONKEY: Double, double, toil and trouble! Hee-haw. Somebody give me an aspirin!

N2: They went on down the road, with both the miller and his son on the donkey…

N1: And a judge and a lawyer happened by.

JUDGE: Would you look at that poor old donkey! Its belly is dragging the ground from the weight of those two perfectly strong and healthy fellows. I call that cruel and unusual punishment.

LAWYER: I agree with your judgment, sir. The two of them look as though *they* should be carrying the donkey. It's only fair.

DONKEY: Hee-haw! What a wonderful idea!

N2: So, the miller and the boy got off the donkey.

N1: And the donkey sat down in the middle of the road to rest.

DONKEY: Oi vay! I'm exhausted. Hee-haw.

MILLER: Son, go over to that tree and get a good strong branch.

DONKEY: Oh no! Now they're going to beat me.

SON: Here's one, Father. Will it do?

MILLER: Yes, it looks sturdy enough. Now let's tie the donkey's feet to the branch.

DONKEY: Tie my feet to the branch? Why are they doing this?

MILLER: Now we'll put the branch across our shoulders.

DONKEY: Helllp! The world looks topsy-turvy!

SON: Oh, I see, Father. Now we can carry the donkey into town.

N2: And there went the donkey—going to market upside down.

DONKEY: Hee-haw! I think I'm gonna be sick.

N1: When they got to town, people stopped and stared.

N2: They had never seen such a sight.

FARMER: That's the silliest thing I've ever laid eyes on!

PEDDLER: Those two fellows don't have a lick of sense.

LAWYER: What's wrong with the donkey? Is he dead?

JUDGE: No, but he soon will be if they don't turn him right side up.

GRANDMA 1: Isn't it a pity that that poor man and his little boy have to carry such a huge burden?

GRANDMA 2: They should have known a donkey wouldn't have sense enough to walk into town on its own two feet.

N1: Meanwhile, the donkey was feeling miserable.

DONKEY: Boy, am I miserable! Hee-haw.

N2: And he was upset by all the noise.

DONKEY: Not to mention that I have an awful headache from my head hitting every bump in the road.

N1:   The donkey began to struggle and wiggle.

MILLER: Hey! Cut that out!

DONKEY: I'm getting out of here. Hee-haw!

SON: Uh-oh. I don't think I can hold on to the branch any longer.

N2:   At that moment, they had just stepped on to a bridge that led into the market.

N1:   The donkey got one foot loose and kicked hard.

SON: Ouch! That hurts.

N2:   The boy dropped his end of the branch. The donkey's other three feet came loose.

N1:   And he rolled off the bridge and into the river.

MILLER: Help! Help! Our donkey can't swim!

DONKEY: Hee-haw! Glub, glub, glub!

N2:   Before anybody could drag the donkey out of the water, he drowned.

SON: Oh, our poor old donkey.

MILLER: Son, we've learned a lesson the hard way today.

N1:   If you try to please everyone…

N2:   You will please no one.

DONKEY: Hee-haw!

Barbara McBride-Smith

Henny Penny
A Traditional Folktale with a Non-Traditional Ending
Scripted for Story Theatre by Barbara McBride-Smith

Cast of eight:

NARRATOR 1 (N1)	DUCKY LUCKY
NARRATOR 2 (N2)	GOOSEY POOSEY
HENNY PENNY	TURKEY LURKEY
COCKY LOCKY	FOXY LOXY

N1: One day, Henny Penny was scratching in the farmyard, when an acorn fell from an oak tree and struck her on the head.

N2: Thunk!

HENNY: Goodness gracious me! The sky is falling! I must go and tell the king the sky is falling!

N2: So, she went along and she went along and she went along, until she met Cocky Locky.

COCKY: Cock-a-doodle-doo! Where are you going in such a hurry, Henny Penny?

HENNY: The sky is falling! The sky is falling! And I am going to tell the king.

COCKY: May I come with you, Henny Penny?

HENNY: Yes, indeed. Come along.

N1: So, Henny Penny and Cocky Locky went off to tell the king that the sky was falling.

N2: They went along and went along and went along, until they met Ducky Lucky.

DUCKY: Quack, quack! Where are you going, Henny Penny and Cocky Locky?

COCKY: The sky is falling! The sky is falling! And we are going to tell the king.

DUCKY: May I come with you?

HENNY:	Yes, indeed. Come along.
N1:	So, Henny Penny and Cocky Locky and Ducky Lucky went off to tell the king that the sky was falling.
N2:	They went along and went along and went along, until they met Goosey Poosey.
GOOSEY:	Honk! Honk! Where are you going, Henny Penny, Cocky Locky, and Ducky Lucky?
DUCKY:	The sky is falling! The sky is falling! And we are going to tell the king.
GOOSEY:	May I come with you?
HENNY:	Yes, indeed. Come along.
N1:	So, Henny Penny, Cocky Locky, Ducky Lucky, and Goosey Poosey went off to tell the king that the sky was falling.
N2:	They went along and went along and went along, until they met Turkey Lurkey.
TURKEY:	Gobble, gobble! Where are you going, Henny Penny, Cocky Locky, Ducky Lucky, and Goosey Poosey?
GOOSEY:	The sky is falling! The sky is falling! And we are going to tell the king.
TURKEY:	May I come with you?
HENNY:	Yes, indeed. Come along.
N1:	So, Henny Penny, Cocky Locky, Ducky Lucky, Goosey Poosey, and Turkey Lurkey went off to tell the king the sky was falling.
N2:	They went along and went along and went along, until they met Foxy Loxy.
FOXY:	Hello, my tasty little friends. Where are you going in such a hurry?
TURKEY:	The sky is falling! The sky is falling! And we are going to tell the king.
FOXY:	The sky is falling? This is a serious situation. And it's a long, long way to the king. But I can help you.

Barbara McBride-Smith

HENNY:	How can you help us, Foxy Loxy?
FOXY:	I know a shortcut to the king's palace.
COCKY:	A shortcut?
FOXY:	Yes, indeed. The king lives on the other side of that big hill. Follow me, and we'll go *through* that hill. We'll get there in half the time.
DUCKY:	*Through* the hill?
FOXY:	Yes, *through* the hill. My den is on the side of that hill. And inside my den, there is a tunnel that goes right through the hill to the other side. Come along and I'll show you.
GOOSEY:	Honk! Honk! You lead the way, Foxy Loxy, and we'll follow.
N1:	So, that sly old fox led Henny Penny, Cocky Locky, Ducky Lucky, Goosey Poosey, and Turkey Lurkey to the entrance of his den.
FOXY:	The secret tunnel through the hill is very narrow, so I'll have to lead you through one at a time. Turkey Lurkey, you come first. I'll be back for each of you. *(chuckles to himself)* Heh, heh, heh.
TURKEY:	Gobble, gobble. It's dark in here.
FOXY:	Don't be afraid, my fat feathered friend. I'll take care of you.
N2:	So, Turkey Lurkey and Foxy Loxy disappeared into the den.
TURKEY:	Gobble, gobble. Gobble, gahhhhhhhh!
N1:	Meanwhile, Henny Penny, Cocky Locky, Ducky Lucky, and Goosey Poosey waited for Foxy Loxy to return.
N2:	Before long, Foxy Loxy came walking out of his den, looking very pleased.
FOXY:	You're next, Goosey Poosey.
GOOSEY:	Me, already?
FOXY:	Don't be afraid. I'll lead the way. Here we go.
GOOSEY:	Honk, honk. Honk, honnnnnnnnk!

N1:	Before long, Foxy Loxy came walking out of his den, looking very pleased.
FOXY:	Your turn, Ducky Lucky. Hurry along, no time to waste.
DUCKY:	Very well, if I must. Quack, quack...Quack, quawwwwk!
N2:	Before long, Foxy Loxy came walking out of his den, looking very pleased.
FOXY:	Three down and two to go. Cocky Locky, come with me. Before you know it, we'll be at the king's palace.
COCKY:	Oh, yes, I must be brave. Cock-a-doodle-doo. Cock-a-doodle-diiiiiiiie!!!
N1:	Henny Penny was all alone now. She waited for Foxy Loxy to return. Suddenly, something fell from a tree and hit the ground beside her.
N2:	Thunk!
HENNY:	Oh, dear! The sky is still falling! I hope we reach the king in time.
N1:	She looked up just as another acorn came tumbling down.
N2:	Thunk!
HENNY:	An acorn! An acorn? Oh dear, do you suppose? Why, the sky is not falling at all. It's only acorns falling. I must tell my friends. My friends will be...oh, no!
N1:	Henny Penny was very suspicious. She walked very quietly to the door of the den and stuck her head inside...
N2:	And what she saw was Foxy Loxy stuffing Cocky Locky into a big bag.
HENNY:	Oh, my poor friends! Shortcut indeed! Oh, what shall I do?
N1:	Henny Penny began to run around the oak tree, trying to think of a plan to save her friends from that wicked fox.
N2:	Another acorn fell from the tree.
N1:	Thunk!

N2:	And another.
N1:	Thunk!
HENNY:	Oh, goodness gracious me. I know what I can do!
N2:	In a flash, Henny Penny flew up into the big oak tree. She gathered all the acorns she could hold. Then she flapped herself to the end of a branch that hung over the entrance to Foxy Loxy's den. She waited…
N1:	And waited…
N2:	And before long, Foxy Loxy came walking out of his den, looking very pleased.
FOXY:	Yoo-hoo, Henny Penny! Where are you, my little chick-a-dee? It's your turn!
N1:	There was no answer. But suddenly…
N2:	Thunk! Whack! Crash! Bam!
N1:	Henny Penny began dropping all those acorns on the fox's head.
N2:	Thunk! Whack! Crash! Bam!
FOXY:	Helllllp! The sky is falling! The sky is falling!
N1:	Foxy Loxy ran as fast as he could, around the tree, over the hill, and out of sight.
N2:	And he was never seen in those parts again.
N1:	Henny Penny hurried into the fox's den to free her four friends.
ALL 4:	*(at the same time)* Cock-a-doodle-doo…Quack, quack…Honk, honk…Gobble, gobble!
DUCKY:	Oh, Henny Penny, it's so good to see you.
GOOSEY:	It's dark in here.
N1:	They hurried out of the den and went along and went along the road back to the farmyard.
N2:	And they all laughed uproariously when they heard how Foxy Loxy had been fooled into thinking that the sky was falling.

HENNY: The sky is falling…indeed! What a silly idea!

N1: *(each animal stands as name is said)* And Henny Penny, Cocky Locky, Ducky Lucky, Goosey Poosey, and Turkey Lurkey…

N2: All lived happily ever after.

Three Billy Goats Gruff: Poetry-Style

A Norwegian Folktale

Scripted in Verse by Barbara McBride-Smith

Cast of six: NARRATOR 1 (N1)   GOAT 1
                NARRATOR 2 (N2)   GOAT 2
                TROLL   GOAT 3

N1 & N2:   Now, once upon a time
                A long time ago,
                There were three billy goats,
                Their name was Gruff, you know.

GOAT 1:   The first billy goat
                Was tiny and cute.
                He wore a pink bow tie
                And a little blue suit.

GOAT 2:   The second billy goat
                Was middle size.
                He wore jeans and boots,
                Just like you guys.

GOAT 3:   The third billy goat
                Was big and strong.
                Wore a black leather jacket,
                And his horns were long.

N1 & N2:   Well, the three billy goats,
                They ate and they ate.
                And the grass disappeared
                At a very fast rate.

N1:   Just across the river
                On the other side,
                There was lots more grass,
                But my, oh my!

TROLL: Underneath that bridge
There lived a troll.
He was ugly and mean,
And his heart was cold.

He had beady red eyes,
And warts on his nose.
He had long sharp teeth,
And hairy old toes.

N1: Well, he owned that bridge,
Or so he thought.

N2: If you tried to walk across,
You were sure to get caught.

GOAT 1: Said the little billy goat,
I'll give it a try.
I'll cross that bridge,
And I'll act real shy.

N1: Trip-trap, trip-trap,
Went his little bitty feet.

TROLL: *Who's a-crossin my bridge?*
Oh, I repeat,

Who's a-crossin my bridge?
Oh, who would dare?
I'll gobble you down
When I get up there!

GOAT 1: *Oh no, not me,*
Said the littlest goat.
I'm bony and thin,
I wouldn't fill your throat.

Just wait a little bit,
And you will see,
A middle-size goat,
Much bigger than me.

Barbara McBride-Smith

TROLL: *Very well*, said the Troll.
          I'll wait just a while.
          When he comes along,
          I'll eat in style.

GOAT 1:   So, the little billy goat,
          He walked on past.
          He crossed that bridge.
          Trip-trapped real fast.

GOAT 2:   Said the second billy goat:
          I'll give it a try.
          I'll cross that bridge,
          And I'll act real sly.

N1:   Trip-trap, trip-trap,
          Went his middle-size feet.

TROLL: *Who's a-crossin my bridge?*
          Oh, I repeat,

          Who's a-crossin my bridge?
          Oh, who would dare?
          I'll gobble you down,
          When I get up there!

GOAT 2:   *Oh no, not me,*
          Said the middle-size kid,
          If you eat me up,
          You'll be sorry you did.

          Just wait a little bit,
          And you will see,
          My big brother goat,
          Much fatter than me.

TROLL: *Very well*, said the Troll,
          I'll wait just a while,
          And when he comes along,
          I'll eat in style.

GOAT 2:
So, the middle billy goat,
He walked on past.
He crossed that bridge,
Trip-trapped real fast.

GOAT 3:
Said the big billy goat,
I'll give it a try.
If he messes with me,
He's a-gonna cry!

N1:
Trip-trap, trip-trap,
Went his big ol' feet.

TROLL:
Who's a-crossin my bridge?
Oh, I repeat,

Who's a crossin my bridge?
Oh, who would dare?
I'll gobble you down,
When I get up there!

GOAT 3:
Well, come on up!
Don't you gimme no lip.
I'm big and I'm mean,
I'm cool and I'm hip.

My horns are sharp,
Do you wanna see?
My hooves can kick,
Just try to gobble me!

N2:
So, up came the Troll,
And the big goat Gruff,
He grabbed that Troll,
And he did his stuff.

N1:
He poked Mr. Troll,
And gave him a lick,
Then punted him high,
With a strong drop kick.

Barbara McBride-Smith

N2:   Ker-splash went the Troll,
         Right into the water.
         You could hear him groan,
         And you could hear him holler.

N1:   Well, he floated away,
         And he never came back.
         Now the bridge is quite safe,
         And that's a fact.

GOAT 3: And the big billy goat,
         He walked on proud,
         He crossed that bridge,
         He trip-trapped loud.

N1 & N2: So the three billy goats,
         Went up the hill,
         And if the grass is green,
         They're up there still.

GOATS 1, 2, 3: *Well, a-hidey-hey,*
                And a-hidey-ho,
                The good guys win,

TROLL: *And the bad guys go!*

N1:   Good-bye, so long,
         With a snip, snap, snout.

N2:   This story is done,
         This tale's told out.

Cat-Skins

A Traditional Folktale from Germany
via the Appalachian Mountains

Scripted for Story Theatre by Barbara McBride-Smith

Cast of seven: NARRATOR 1 (N1)   COOK
                              NARRATOR 2 (N2)   GIRL
                              CAT-SKINS   SON
                              OLD MAN

N1: Once upon a time, there was a young orphan girl who lived on a farm with an old man and an old woman.

N2: The old man and the old woman made that poor girl work hard every day, and they never paid her a penny.

CAT-SKINS: All I've got to wear is this faded old flour-sack dress. It's got so many holes in it, I might just as well be wearing a fish net. Wonder what they've got around here that I can use to patch up this dress?

N1: Well, about all they had plenty of around that house was cobwebs and cat hair.

N2: You see, that old woman loved cats. She had about a hundred of 'em.

CAT-SKINS: And when one of those cats died, she couldn't bring herself to bury it. So she'd just leave it lying on the floor or on the bed or in the windowsill—wherever it was when it passed on. And after a month or two, there wouldn't be any cat left inside. Just the skin and hair would be lying there.

N1: So that girl began to use those cat pelts to patch her raggedy dress.

N2: Finally, her whole dress was nothing but cat skins. Cat skins all over. It had cat ears sticking out here, and cat tails dangling off there.

CAT-SKINS: I know it doesn't smell so nice, but it keeps me warm and covered.

N1:   Besides, it was an interesting fashion statement.

N2:   But would you believe, that girl never had a single boyfriend?

CAT-SKINS: Anyway, that's how I got my name—Cat-Skins.

N1:   One day the old woman took sick and died.

CAT-SKINS: I was worried that the old man would just leave the old woman lying there in the bed until nothing was left but her skin. So I took the old woman out to the yard and buried her under a magnolia tree.

N2:   The next day the old man found the old woman's will in her lock-box.

OLD MAN: Look here, Cat-Skins. The old woman didn't have much to leave behind. Her share of the farm goes to the cats. And her wedding dress goes to you. I reckon you can wash it and wear it whenever you're a mind to.

N1:   So Cat-Skins laundered that dress and put it on the very next day.

OLD MAN: Glory be, Cat-Skins! You smell so fresh and look so pretty, I didn't recognize you without those feline tails floppin' around all over you. How about if we get married?

CAT-SKINS: Well, I'll think about it. But first, you've got to buy me a dress the color of all the fish that swim in the sea.

OLD MAN: You find it in the mail order catalog, and I'll buy it for you.

N2:   It seems as how that old man had more money than anybody knew about.

N2:   So he ordered a dress that was all the colors of the fish in the sea.

CAT-SKINS: This is a mighty pretty dress! Thank you!

OLD MAN: I'm glad you like it. Now will you marry me?

CAT-SKINS: I'll think about it. But first, you've got to buy me a dress the color of all the birds that fly in the sky.

N1:   So he ordered her a dress that was all the colors of the birds that fly in the sky.

Barbara McBride-Smith

CAT-SKINS:	This is a mighty pretty dress! Thank you, again!
OLD MAN:	You're welcome. Now will you marry me?
CAT-SKINS:	I'll think about it. But first, you've got to buy me a dress the color of all the flowers that grow in the world.
N2:	So he ordered her a calico dress that was all the colors of the flowers in the world.
CAT-SKINS:	Oh, it's beautiful! Thank you, thank you, thank you!
OLD MAN:	You're welcome three times. Now will you marry me?
CAT-SKINS:	I'll think about it. But first, I'd like to go for a ride in your flying machine.
OLD MAN:	How did you find out about my flying machine?
CAT-SKINS:	Oh, I was cleaning in the barn one day, and I came upon it under a pile of cat hair.
OLD MAN:	I won that flying machine in a card game a long time ago. I've been saving it for a special trip someday. Hmmm. I reckon I could let you take a little spin in the air.
CAT-SKINS:	That would make me mighty happy.
OLD MAN:	All right, then. You can take it up. But don't get any scratches on it. And hurry back, so we can get married. I'll send a message to the preacher in town to come on up here today.
N1:	Soon as the old man was out of sight, Cat-Skins pulled that flying machine out to the front yard and put all her new dresses in it.
N2:	Then she jumped in, fastened her seatbelt, and hollered:
CAT-SKINS:	Fly real high! Up to the sky!
N1:	The flying machine rose way up into the air, and Cat-Skins flew as far from that farm as she could go.
N2:	After a while, she looked down, and she saw a big white mansion surrounded by a perfectly manicured lawn of green grass and a flowerbed of brightly colored roses.

CAT-SKINS:	Goodness gracious! I reckon I'm not in Appalachia any more.
N1:	Cat-Skins was so curious about that big house, she decided to have a closer look.
CAT-SKINS:	Take me down! Soft to the ground!
N2:	The flying machine landed in the grass, and Cat-Skins pushed it behind a bush to hide it.
N1:	Then she walked up to that big fancy house and knocked at the back door.
SOUND:	Knock-knock!
N2:	She was wearing her dress made of cat pelts, so the woman who opened the door was taken by surprise.
COOK:	Mercy! Who are you and what's that smelly thing you're wearing?
CAT-SKINS:	My name is Cat-Skins and that's also what I'm wearing. I need a job.
COOK:	You think I'd let an odd-looking thing like you stay around this house? You'd have every dog in the neighborhood barking its fool head off.
GIRL:	Don't be so hard-hearted, Cookie. I think she looks like an adventuresome person. My daddy owns this house, and I say she can stay!
N1:	So Cat-Skins went to work in the kitchen of that big house, picking the chickens and chopping the livers.
N2:	At first, the other kitchen folks were scared of her. They thought she was some kind of varmint with too many ears and tails. But after a few days, they got used to her.
N1:	One night, the rich man who owned that house was having a fancy party. Cat-Skins was helping the man's daughter get dressed in her party clothes.
CAT-SKINS:	You sure do look pretty. I reckon all the boys will want to dance with you.

Barbara McBride-Smith

GIRL: All the boys, except my brother. He says I'm a pain in the neck. He's a pain in the neck, too. He's old enough to get married and leave home, but he can't find a girl good enough to suit him.

CAT-SKINS: Is he looking for a pretty girl or a smart girl?

GIRL: Both! Hey, Cat-Skins, have you ever seen a fancy ball? You ought to come around to the ballroom windows tonight and peek in. You can see for yourself how snooty my brother acts.

CAT-SKINS: Well, I might do that…and I might not.

N2: Later that night, Cat-Skins went out to the yard and found the flying machine she had hidden behind a bush.

N1: She took out the dress that was the color of all the fish in the sea and put it on.

CAT-SKINS: Now I believe I'll take a peek at that fancy party.

N2: She walked right into that party just like she belonged there. She was so beautiful she nearly took everybody's breath away.

SON: Hello there! Welcome to my daddy's house. You must be new around here. Care to dance?

CAT-SKINS: Thank you. I'd love to dance.

N1: They danced together all evening. They waltzed and jitter-bugged and tangoed. And as the hour was getting late, they did the Virginia Reel, and Cat-Skins do-si-doed right out the door.

N2: She ran to the flying machine, hid the colorful dress inside it, and went back to the kitchen wearing her old cat-skins dress.

N1: The next day, the rich man's daughter came down to the kitchen.

GIRL: Cat-Skins! Did you peek in the ballroom window last night?

CAT-SKINS: Sort of.

GIRL: Did you see that pretty girl in that gorgeous dress?

CAT-SKINS: Yep, I saw her.

GIRL: Do you think my brother liked her?

CAT-SKINS: Maybe. Maybe not.

GIRL: Well, he asked my daddy to give another party tonight. I suspect he's hoping she'll come back. Will you be peeking in the windows to see what happens?

CAT-SKINS: I might do that…and I might not.

N2: Sure enough, Cat-Skins helped that girl get ready for the ball that night. Then she went out to the yard and opened up the flying machine.

CAT-SKINS: Let's see. Tonight I'll wear the dress that's all the colors of the birds in the sky.

N1: She went walking into the party like she was as good as anybody there.

SON: Welcome back, ma'am. That sure is a beautiful dress. Would you like to dance?

CAT-SKINS: Yes, thank you. I'd be happy to dance with you.

N2: Cat-Skins and that boy had a fine evening. But when he went to get her some punch, she slipped out the door.

N1: She put the dress back into the flying machine, wrapped her cat-skins around herself, and was back in the kitchen before midnight.

GIRL: Good morning, Cat-Skins! Did you see that mysterious girl at the party last night.

CAT-SKINS: Yep, I saw her.

GIRL: That dress was spectacular. Looked like it was the color of…

CAT-SKINS: All the birds that fly in the sky?

GIRL: That's it! All the birds that fly in the sky! And did you see how my brother danced every dance with her?

CAT-SKINS: Yep, I saw that, too.

GIRL: Well, I think he's stuck on her. He has asked Daddy to throw another party tonight. Cat-Skins, why don't you borrow one of my dresses and come to the party so you can see what happens?

COOK:	Humpf! You better not let that dirty girl put one of your dresses on herself. You'll get fleas!
CAT-SKINS:	Thank you for offering me a dress. But I wouldn't feel right at such a fine affair. Maybe I'll just watch from the window… maybe not.
N2:	That night when the party got started, Cat-Skins ran out to the flying machine and took out her calico dress—the one that was the colors of all the flowers in the world.
N1:	She put it on and went to the party.
SON:	Hi there! I've been hoping you'd come. Shall we dance?
N2:	That dress was so radiant, and the couple looked so perfect together, everybody just ooh-ed and ahh-ed about 'em all evening.
CAT-SKINS:	I am having the best time of my life, but could we sit down and rest for a minute?
SON:	I'm glad you asked, because I've got a little gift for you.
N1:	Before Cat-Skins could catch her breath, that boy slipped a ring on her finger.
CAT-SKINS:	Oh my! What a surprise! I've got to go!
N2:	Cat-Skins ran outside, hid her dress and the ring in the flying machine, slipped back into her cat-skin dress, and was sitting in the kitchen when the girl came running in to find her.
GIRL:	Oooh, Cat-Skins! Were you there tonight?
CAT-SKINS:	Yep, I was there.
GIRL:	I never saw you.
CAT-SKINS:	Well, I saw you.
GIRL:	How about the dress that strange girl was wearing tonight! Did you ever see anything like it before?
CAT-SKINS:	Maybe once or twice.

GIRL:	Well, you won't see it again. My daddy says he's not giving any more parties. And my brother is worried sick that he'll never find out who that mysterious girl is.
CAT-SKINS:	What a shame.
N1:	The next day that rich man's son started hunting for the girl who wore the three beautiful dresses. When he couldn't find her, he took to his sickbed and wouldn't eat.
N2:	He said he'd die if he didn't find that girl.
COOK:	I'll make him some of my best kidney pie. He's never been able to resist it.
SON:	No thank you. Take it away.
GIRL:	I'll fix him some fried gizzards. They're a fine delicacy.
SON:	No thank you. I really can't eat anything.
CAT-SKINS:	How about if I bake him a cake?
COOK:	*You* bake him a cake?! He really would get sick if you was to bake him anything!
GIRL:	Aw, Cookie, don't be so unkind. Let Cat-Skins bake him a cake if she wants to.
N1:	So Cat-Skins slipped out and got that ring, and when she baked the cake, she put the ring in it. The she covered it all over with fluffy white icing.
CAT-SKINS:	I reckon I'll take this cake up to that poor sick boy now.
COOK:	You ugly thing! You can't go up there in them old cat-hides. You'll make him sicker than ever if he has to look at them things!
N2:	So the cook traipsed up to the boy's room and cut him a piece of the cake.
SOUND:	Ping!
N1:	The ring fell out on the plate.
SON:	Who baked this cake?

COOK:	I did! I baked it just for you!
SON:	No such thing! You go get whoever *did* bake it and bring her here right now!
N2:	The cook fetched Cat-Skins and sent her up there in a hurry.
CAT-SKINS:	Hello. Did you like my cake?
SON:	I don't know about the cake, but I sure like *you.*
CAT-SKINS:	Even in my cat-skins dress?
SON:	Clothes don't make the woman.
CAT-SKINS:	You're right about that. Meow! *(both laugh)*
SON:	Will you marry me?
CAT-SKINS:	Maybe. How do you feel about flying?
SON:	I've always wanted to fly!
CAT-SKINS:	Then I reckon I'll marry you.
N1:	So Cat-Skins and the rich man's son got married that very day.
CAT-SKINS:	Fly real high! Up to the sky!
N2:	And as far as anybody knows, they're still traveling all over the world in their wonderful flying machine.

FICTION

Bubba the Cowboy Prince

From the book by Helen Ketteman
*Bubba the Cowboy Prince**

Adapted for Story Theatre by Barbara McBride-Smith

Cast of eight:
NARRATOR 1 (N1) STEPDADDY (SD)
NARRATOR 2 (N2) DWAYNE
BUBBA MILTON
MIZ LURLEEN (MIZ L) FAIRY GODCOW (COW)

N1: Once upon a time, way out in west Texas, there lived a strapping young feller named Bubba.

BUBBA: Howdy! I'm Bubba.

N2: Bubba lived on a ranch with his wicked stepdaddy...

SD: Wicked? What do you mean "wicked"?

N2: And his two hateful and lazy stepbrothers...

DWAYNE: Hi! I'm Dwayne. I ain't lazy. I just don't move too fast.

MILTON: And I'm Milton. I'm hateful and proud of it.

N1: Bubba's wicked stepdaddy spoiled Dwayne and Milton no end, but Bubba worked from sunup to sundown doing all the chores around the ranch.

N2: But Bubba never complained. He loved ranching.

BUBBA: You bet your boots! I do love ranchin'!

N1: Dwayne and Milton spent their days settin' on horseback, bossing Bubba around.

DWAYNE: Git them dogies along there, Bubba.

MILTON: Yeah, and watch out fer them cowpatties. You know how Daddy hates fer you to track up the house with them things.

BUBBA: Thanks for the advice, fellers. I'll be done here real soon. And then I'll git your supper cooked.

* *Bubba the Cowboy Prince* by Helen Ketteman (Scholastic, 1997). Adapted with permission from Curtis Brown, Ltd., Ten Astor Place, New York, NY 10003.

N2:   Now, down the road a piece, there lived the purtiest and the richest gal in the county. She owned the biggest spread of land west of the Brazos River.

N1:   Her name was Miz Lurleen, and she loved ranchin' a whole bunch. But it was lonesome work, and after a while, she decided it was time for some companionship.

MIZ L: I aim to find myself a feller. One who loves ranching as much as I do. And it wouldn't hurt if he was cute as a cow's ear either.

N2:   Miz Lurleen decided to throw a ball—a real Texas hoedown. She sent out invitations to all the ranchers in Texas.

N1:   When the day of the ball arrived, Milton and Dwayne spent all day getting gussied up in their finest duds. Bubba just about run hisself ragged a'waitin' on 'em.

DWAYNE: Bubba! Fetch my bolo tie…and hurry up!

MILTON: Bubba! Git my boots polished…and make it snappy!

SD: Bubba! Brush them horses and wash that wagon!

BUBBA: Yessir. I'll try to work a little faster.

N2:   By the time Dwayne and Milton and the wicked stepdaddy were ready to go, Bubba was exhausted. The three of 'em climbed into the wagon and started down the road.

BUBBA: Can't you wait just a little bit while I git ready? I want to dance with Miz Lurleen, too.

SD: *You?* Why, you're sorrier than a steer in a stockyard. *(laughing)*

DWAYNE: Miz Lurleen ain't gonna dance with the likes of you. She wouldn't even wipe the dirt clods off her boots with that raggedy shirt of yours.

MILTON: You smell more like the cattle than the cattle do!

N1:   Bubba took a look at himself.

BUBBA: It's true. I don't have a decent shirt to wear, and my boots are downright disgraceful. I reckon I do smell a bit rough. Them fellers are right. Miz Lurleen wouldn't dance with the likes of me. Oh, woe is me…I feel lower than a rattlesnake in a ditch.

N2: Milton and Dwayne and the wicked stepdaddy went on down the road to the ball. Bubba mounted his horse and headed for the pasture to check on the cattle.

N1: The sky was getting darker than a black bull at midnight. It sure enough looked like a Texas thunderstorm was brewing.

N2: Bubba had just arrived at the cow pasture, when...*Blam!*...

N1: A bolt of lightning struck, knocking him off his horse.

N2: Bubba was stunned for a minute, but as he was picking himself up off the ground, he heard a voice.

COW: Go to the ball, Bubba.

BUBBA: Who said that? I don't see anybody...but me...and the cows. Now hold on just a minute! Did I knock the bejeebers out of my brains, or is one of you a talkin' cow?

COW: Don't worry, Bubba. You're not crazy. I am your fairy godcow. And I can help you go to the ball.

BUBBA: Oh, Miz Godcow, I'd sure like to go. But shoot, I don't have a thing to wear.

N1: The fairy godcow swished her tail, and Bubba's raggedy clothes changed into the handsomest cowboy duds he'd ever laid eyes on.

N2: His jeans were crisp, his boots were shiny, his shirt was dazzling, and his Stetson was whiter than a new salt lick.

BUBBA: Whoopee! I look downright purty, don't I?

N1: The fairy godcow swished her tail again, and a nearby steer turned into the most beautiful white stallion Bubba had ever seen.

COW: Now you go on to the ball, Bubba. Have a good time dancing with Miz Lurleen. But you gotta come on home by midnight, Bubba, 'cause that's when the magic runs out.

BUBBA: Yes, ma'am! And thank you, Miz Godcow. Yahoo!

N2: When Bubba arrived at Miz Lurleen's ranch, the hoedown was in full swing.

N1:	But, so far, Miz Lurleen was not impressed with any of the fellers she had danced with that night.
MIZ L:	Well, there goes another ten-dollar hat on a five-cent head. Where are all the *real* cowboys?
N2:	By the time it was Bubba's turn to dance with Miz Lurleen, it was almost midnight.
N1:	As soon as she saw Bubba, her eyes lit up.
MIZ L:	Well, hi there, stranger! You're cute as a cow's ear. You wanna dance?
BUBBA:	Aw shucks, ma'am. I reckon I do.
N2:	When Dwayne and Milton saw that handsome stranger dancing with Miz Lurleen…
N1:	And when they saw how she was smilin' at him…
N2:	They turned purple with jealousy.
DWAYNE:	Who is that dude, anyhow?
MILTON:	I don't recollect ever seein' him before, but somehow he looks a mite bit familiar.
SD:	Do something, boys! That shiny lookin' cowboy is winnin' Miz Lurleen's heart.
MILTON:	Maybe we can start a fight with him.
DWAYNE:	Aw shoot, I don't like fightin'. I might git hurt.
N1:	But all of a sudden…
COW:	Bong! Bong! Bong! Bong! *(continue up to twelve)*
N2:	Suddenly, Bubba's fine duds turned into the dirty rags he usually wore around the ranch. He looked sorry…
N1:	And he smelled worse.
DWAYNE:	Aw gag! What is that awful smell?
MILTON:	Why, lookie there! It's Bubba!

SD: Well, I'll be danged! And don't he look purty standin' there turnin' fourteen shades of red? Haw, haw!

BUBBA: Uh-oh, I should have paid attention to the time. I'm a mess! Miz Lurleen, forgive me, but I gotta be goin'.

N2: Bubba took off running, and Miz Lurleen started to chase him.

MIZ L: Wait a minute, cowboy! Don't go. I don't even know your name!

N1: But Bubba didn't wait. He jumped on his cow and headed off into the night.

N2: In the ruckus, however, Bubba lost one of his dirty cowboy boots.

MIZ L: Well now, look at this. This is the boot of a real cowboy. I aim to find him and marry him…if he'll have me, that is.

N1: Miz Lurleen went back inside and asked everybody at the ball if they knew who the mysterious cowboy was.

N2: Nobody did.

SD: *(stage whisper)* Well, actually, WE *do know* who he is, but we ain't talkin'.

N1: The next day, Miz Lurleen went from ranch to ranch, looking for the cowboy who owned the boot.

N2: When she came to the wicked stepdaddy's ranch, both Dwayne and Milton tried to put that boot on.

MILTON: Gimme that boot. I'm sure it's mine. Oh doggone-it, my foot must be swollen up from dancing last night.

DWAYNE: Here, let me try. So what if it's a mite bit too big. I'll just stick a sock down in the toe. Yep, it's mine, all right.

MIZ L: Sorry, boys. But I don't believe this here boot belongs to either one of you. Reckon I'll just have to keep on searching for my cowboy.

N1: About that time, Bubba came riding up. He was dirty and sweaty and smelly from working with the cows.

N2: And he was wearing only *one* boot.

MIZ L: Well, howdy-do. How about if you try this boot on?

BUBBA: Much obliged, ma'am. Well, what do you know? It fits. And it matches my other one.

MIZ L: You're my prince in cowboy boots! I'd recognize that smell anywhere! Marry me, cowboy, and help me work my ranch!

BUBBA: Aw shucks, ma'am. Well…OK, I think I will. I just love ranchin'!

N1:   Dwayne and Milton and the wicked stepdaddy threw chicken fits.

DWAYNE: Dad-gummit! It ain't fair!

MILTON: No siree! It just ain't fair!

SD: Oh, hush up, you hateful and lazy good-fer-nothin's! Life ain't supposed to be fair! Otherwise, I wouldn't have got stuck with you two!

N2:   Bubba just smiled, and he and Miz Lurleen rode off into the sunset.

N1:   And they lived happily ever after…

N2:   A-ridin'

N1:   And a-ropin'

N2:   And a-gittin' them dogies along.

COW: Moooo!

Barbara McBride-Smith

Little Red Cowboy Hat

From the book by Susan Lowell
Little Red Cowboy Hat*

Adapted for Story Theatre by Barbara McBride-Smith

Cast of seven:
NARRATOR 1 (N1)	WOLF
NARRATOR 2 (N2)	GRANDMA
LITTLE RED (RED)	SOUND
MOTHER	

N1: Once upon a ranch, far away in the wild, wild West, there lived a little girl with red, red hair.

N2: Her hair was a color of red somewhere between firecrackers and new pennies.

N1: And to top it off, her grandmother gave her a bright red cowboy hat.

N2: So everybody called her Little Red Cowboy Hat.

N1: Or just plain Little Red, for short.

N2: One day her mama said…

MOTHER: Little Red, your dear Grandma's sick in bed. Saddle up your pony and ride over to your Grandma's house, and take her this loaf of my homemade sourdough bread and a jar of my cactus jelly.

N1: Little Red loved to visit her grandma.

RED: Yes, ma'am!

MOTHER: And don't dilly-dally along the way.

RED: Yes, ma'am!

MOTHER: And be careful. Look out for rattlesnakes.

RED: Yes, ma'am!

N2: Little Red saddled up her pony, packed the loaf of bread and jar of jelly in her saddlebag, and set off for her grandma's ranch.

---

* *Little Red Cowboy Hat* by Susan Lowell. (Henry Holt, 1997). Adapted with permission from Jean V. Naggar Literary Agency, 216 W. 75th Street, New York, NY 10021.

SOUND:	Clippety-clop, clippety-clop.
N1:	First she rode down into a deep canyon.
SOUND:	Clippety-clop, clippety-clop.
N2:	Then she rode up onto a wide mesa where the bluebonnets were in full bloom.
SOUND:	Clippety-clop, clippety-clop.
RED:	Oooh, Grandma loves bluebonnets. I'll stop for just a minute and pick her a bouquet.
SOUND:	Clippety-clop. Whoa!
N1:	As she was picking the flowers, she heard her pony give a whinny.
SOUND:	Neighhhhh!
RED:	What's wrong, Buckskin? Is it a snake?
N2:	Suddenly, out from behind a mesquite bush popped a wolf.
WOLF:	Howdy, little girl. *(WOLF tips his black hat to LITTLE RED)*
RED:	Howdy. *(LITTLE RED tips her red hat to WOLF)*
N1:	Little Red really didn't want to talk to the wolf, but her mama had taught her to be polite.
WOLF:	What's your name, little girl?
RED:	Little Red Cowboy Hat. But everybody calls me Little Red.
N2:	Her mama had also taught her to tell the truth.
WOLF:	Red? Red…as in ketchup? Red…as in blood?…uh, I mean, red as in roses?
N1:	A creepy feeling ran up Little Red's spine. Her red hair tingled all the way down to the roots.
N2:	Little Red said to herself…
RED:	This wolf is much too close. I can count the teeth in his smile. I don't believe I can trust him.

Barbara McBride-Smith

WOLF:	You look like a mighty fine horsewoman, honey. How about taking a little ride with me?
SOUND:	Neighhh!
N1:	Buckskin reared up, his front hooves kicking the air.
RED:	Come here, Buckskin! 'Atta boy! Now giddy-up!
N2:	While the wolf was trying to keep from being trampled by the horse's hooves, Little Red jumped on her pony and galloped away.
N1:	When Little Red reached her grandma's ranch, she didn't hear a sound except the windmill creaking.
SOUND:	Skree, skree. Skree, skree.
N2:	The chickens didn't even cluck.
N1:	Nothing moved except three buzzards circling high up in the sky.
RED:	Grandma's usually outside tending the cows or mixing cement. Poor Grandma. She must be *real* sick.
N2:	Little Red tied her pony to the hitching post and tippy-toed into the house.
RED:	*(softly)* Grandma?
N1:	She saw a big lump in her grandma's bed.
N2:	She saw the lacy edge of her grandma's nightcap peeking out from under the patchwork quilt.
RED:	I brought you some homemade bread and jelly, Grandma.
WOLF:	*(muffled voice)* Thank you, honey bun.
SOUND:	Ka-thunk!
RED:	What was that noise outside?
WOLF:	Noise? What noise, dear?
RED:	Grandma, is that really you?
WOLF:	Of course it's me, sweetie.

RED: Why are you all covered up? I can't see you very well.

N1: The lump moved. Deep down in the bed covers, a big dark eye glittered.

RED: Shoot-a-mile, Grandma! You really must be sick. What big dark eyes you have!

WOLF: The better to see you with, pumpkin.

SOUND: Ka-thunk!

RED: There's that noise again! I'm sure it's coming from outside.

WOLF: Don't worry about it, dear.

N2: The quilt slipped off a huge, hairy muzzle.

RED: Oh my, what a big nose you have, Grandma.

WOLF: The better to smell you with, dumpling.

SOUND: Ka-thunk! Ka-thunk!

N1: By now, Little Red knew that something was wrong. She also suspected that this was not her grandma.

RED: Grandma, what sharp teeth you have!

WOLF: The better to eat you with, angel pie!

N2: The wolf sat bolt upright and grabbed Little Red Cowboy Hat.

WOLF: Come here, sweet cakes!

SOUND: Ka-thunk, ka-thunk, ka-thunk!

RED: Help! Help!

WOLF: Be quiet, you delicious little morsel. Yum-yum!

N1: At that very moment, Grandma came charging through the door, with an ax in her hand. She had been outside chopping wood when she heard the commotion in her house.

GRANDMA: Get your paws off my granddaughter, you lousy varmint!

WOLF: Yikes! I'm outta here!

Barbara McBride-Smith

N2:	The wolf dropped Little Red like a hot potato and made a break for the window.
GRANDMA:	Are you all right, Red?
RED:	Yes, ma'am. I'm fine.
N1:	The wolf tripped over his nightgown and got stuck in the window.
N2:	Grandma grabbed her shotgun from the mantel.
SOUND:	Ka-blam!
GRANDMA:	Take that, you low-life lobo!
SOUND:	Ka-blam!
N1:	The wolf pulled himself through the window and took off across Grandma's north forty.
WOLF:	Sorry, ladies, but I really must be running along now!
GRANDMA:	Come on, Red!
N2:	Little Red leaped onto her pony…
N1:	and Grandma leaped onto her stallion…
SOUND:	Neighhh!
N2:	They chased that wolf right through Grandma's herd of longhorns.
SOUND:	Moooo! Moooo!
GRANDMA:	I'll teach you to go breaking into my house!
SOUND:	Ka-blam!
GRANDMA:	Wearing my clothes! Getting fleas in my bed!
SOUND:	Ka-blam!
GRANDMA:	Messing with my granddaughter!
SOUND:	Ka-blam!
GRANDMA:	You'd look mighty good as a rug, Mister Wolf!

SOUND: Ka-blam! Splat!

WOLF: Ai-yi-yi!!!! Ah-oooooo!

N1:   Later, back at the ranch, Little Red Cowboy Hat and her grandma sat down to eat their sourdough bread and cactus jelly.

GRANDMA: Now, Red, have you learned your lesson?

RED: Yes, ma'am. A girl's gotta stick up for herself.

GRANDMA: That's right. And I reckon that wolf learned his lesson, too. That yellow-bellied, snake-blooded, skunk-eyed, rancid son of a parallelogram messed with the wrong grandma this time!

RED: Yes, ma'am!

N2:   And they never had any trouble with wolves around that ranch again.

A Thoroughly Modern Rapunzel

A Story by Jude Mandell,
from Bruce Lansky's *Newfangled Fairy Tales, Book 2* *

Adapted for Story Theatre by Barbara McBride-Smith

Cast of seven:

NARRATOR 1 (N1)	DAD
NARRATOR 2 (N2)	MOM
RAPUNZEL	DOUG TOTO
MESMERELDA	

RAPUNZEL: So there I was, me—Rapunzel—prisoner in a tall apartment building, grounded for life by an evil witch…all because my mom was crazy about pizza!

N1: Here's how it all began…

N2: There was once a witch named Mesmerelda who sold the tastiest pizzas in New York. Her recipe was a secret blend of tomatoes, toadstools, spices, spiders, cheese, crust, and magic spells.

N1: One bite and you were hooked.

RAPUNZEL: My mom and dad lived in a tiny apartment next to Mesmerelda's restaurant. My father was out of work, so they were too poor to buy her pizza.

DAD: But money or no money, we're happy. Aren't we, dear?

MOM: Oh yes, indeed. And I have the most wonderful news. We're going to have a child. I wonder if it will be a boy or a girl?

RAPUNZEL: That's me they're talking about. And of course, I was gonna be a girl.

MESMERELDA: Youse two lovebirds are soooo lucky. I always wanted a brat of my own.

N2: The next day a free sample of Mesmerelda's Magically Delicious Pizza appeared on the young couple's doorstep. A mouth-watering smell drifted from the box.

* "A Thoroughly Modern Rapunzel" by Jude Mandell. From *Newfangled Fairy Tales, Book 2*, edited by Bruce Lansky (Meadowbrook Press, 1998). Adapted with permission from Meadowbrook Press, 5451 Smetana Drive, Minnetonka, MN 55343.

MOM:	Ooooh, look at this, dear. Two slices of pizza. Where do you suppose it came from? Let me try it and see if it's fresh. *(takes a small bite)* Yum-yum! *(gobbles down rest of slice)*
DAD:	Must be good. I guess I'll try this other slice.
MOM:	Hands off! I'm starved! This pizza is mine, all mine!
RAPUNZEL:	No doubt about it—Mom was hooked. The next thing Dad knew she had wrestled him to the ground and snatched his slice of pizza, too.
DAD:	Get a grip, sweetie! I would've given it to you, if you had asked.
MOM:	Sorry, dear. I don't know what came over me. It's like some weird spell hit me.
N1:	From that day on, the mother-to-be craved Mesmerelda's pizza. When the aroma drifted in from next door, drool dribbled down her chin. Soon she refused to eat anything else.
MOM:	Oh, woe is me! I'm starving for a slice of that pizza. Please dear, *get it for me…Now!*
DAD:	Maybe I can scrape together enough money to buy one slice.
N2:	But one slice was never enough.
DAD:	I'll never be able to buy as much pizza as she wants. Maybe when Mesmerelda closes up the shop tonight, I can slip in the back and "borrow" any leftover cold pizza that might be lying around.
RAPUNZEL:	So, that night when Mom was asleep, my poor worried father sneaked into Mesmerelda's kitchen, grabbed a pizza, stripped off the anchovies, and crept toward the door.
MESMERELDA:	What's da matter, thief?! Ya don't like anchovies?!
DAD:	Yikes! Don't sneak up on me like that. You almost gave me a heart attack!
MESMERELDA:	Wait till I call da cops, and dey throw you in jail. Dat won't be too good for your health, either.
DAD:	I'll pay you for the pizza when I get a job, Mesmerelda. Think of it as a loan.

Barbara McBride-Smith

MESMERELDA: Yo! Do I look like a bank? Hand it over, thief.

DAD: But my wife will starve without your pizza. She won't eat anything else!

MESMERELDA: Well, I wouldn't want dat to happen, her havin' da kid and all. Tell ya what. Your wife gets all da pizza she wants, on one condition—I get da kid when it's born.

DAD: Trade our baby for pizzas? No way! How's about if I wash your pizza pans instead and work off what I owe?

MESMERELDA: No dice! No baby, no pizza!

DAD: *(to himself)* What should I do? Maybe I can go along with her on this and eventually get her to change her mind before our child is born. *(to MESMERELDA)* All right. My wife's favorite is pizza topped with rapunzel salad.

MESMERELDA: One rapunzel special comin' up!

RAPUNZEL: As the months went by, Dad had no luck in getting Mesmerelda to change her mind.

MESMERELDA: Nope! It's too late for money. Da only way youse can pay me off is in baby-bucks.

N1: And then the day came when the baby daughter was born.

RAPUNZEL: Waaaaa!

MESMERELDA: Oh goodie, a girl-brat! Thanks! I tink I'll call her Rapunzel—ya know, after da pizza topping. Here's some half-price pizza coupons for youse two. Enjoy!

MOM: Wait just a minute! You can't take our daughter!

DAD: We'll sell everything we own to pay you back.

MESMERELDA: Youse two are gettin' on my nerves!

N2: With a flick of her magic pizza cutter, she changed the two parents into pizza delivery vans. She jumped into one and drove the child to a tall apartment building in a deserted neighborhood.

N1: She sealed the doors and windows of the building with magic spells so that only she could get in and out.

RAPUNZEL: Every day she fed me pizza sauce in baby bottles. When I grew teeth, she gave me regular pizza. Eating nothing but pizza made my hair grow like crazy. It was about a jillion feet long when I turned seven.

MESMERELDA: Seven years old today, eh? You're growin' fast, Rapunzel. Although you ain't really my kid, I'm countin' on you to run my pizza place when I get old. Someday it'll be yours.

RAPUNZEL: What? You mean you're not my mother?

MESMERELDA: Get real, kid. We ain't exactly look-alikes.

RAPUNZEL: I pleaded with her to tell me what had become of my parents. When she told me about the delivery vans, I became very upset.

MESMERELDA: I was afraid she might run away, so I moved her to da top floor of da apartment building. Then I got rid of all da staircases and fire escapes.

RAPUNZEL: But every day, Mesmerelda came to visit me.

MESMERELDA: Yo, Rapunzel! Let down your hair. Pizza delivery.

N2:   Rapunzel would throw her long braids over the balcony, and up Mesmerelda would climb with a pizza box under her arm. Well, Rapunzel put up with this foolishness until her sixteenth birthday. She blew out all the candles on her cake-and-ice-cream pizza and said…

RAPUNZEL: My wish is to be like the kids I see on TV. I want to have friends, go to school, and eat something besides pizza—like hot dogs and french fries and hot fudge sundaes. If you don't promise I can do these things, I'll never let my hair down to you again!

MESMERELDA: I'll teach you to talk back to me!

N1:   Mesmerelda picked up her magic pizza cutter, and *Sha-zam!* She turned Rapunzel into a giant pepperoni sausage with long hair. The spell lasted a whole month.

RAPUNZEL: After that, I knew I had to escape.

N2:   A week later, a young guy came hip-hopping by the apartment building, his boom box blaring. Rapunzel couldn't believe it. Nobody ever came by there.

Barbara McBride-Smith

RAPUNZEL: Yoo-hoo! Hello down there! *(louder)* Hey, fella! Look up here! *(quieter)* Well, sorry to do this, but I've gotta get your attention.

N1: Rapunzel grabbed the nearest pizza and hurled it like a Frisbee.

N2: It hit him—smack!—in the face.

DOUG: Hey! What's the big idea?

RAPUNZEL: Sorry, but I need your help.

N1: The guy scraped the spinach-and-peanut-butter pizza off his face and got a good look at Rapunzel.

DOUG: No problemo, beautiful. You can throw pizza at me anytime.

MESMERELDA: Rapunzel, Rapunzel!

RAPUNZEL: Hide! Here comes the witch who keeps me captive.

N2: The guy ducked into an alley just before Mesmerelda appeared.

MESMERELDA: Yo, Rapunzel! Pizza delivery!

RAPUNZEL: I let down my locks, and up climbed Mesmerelda.

DOUG: And as soon as the old witch left, I climbed up. I found this beautiful girl scratching her head. *(to RAPUNZEL)* What's the matter, beautiful? Cooties?

RAPUNZEL: No! All that pulling on my hair makes my scalp itch.

DOUG: Aw, that's too bad. Why doesn't that old witch just fly up here on her broom?

RAPUNZEL: She doesn't have a broom. Besides, flying makes her throw up.

DOUG: Sorry I asked. My name is Doug Toto. Are you old enough to date? You like to dance?

RAPUNZEL: One step at a time. First I need your help to escape from this boring apartment.

DOUG: I've got that figured out already. Be ready to leave at daybreak.

N1: That night, Mesmerelda took so long climbing up Rapunzel's hair, Rapunzel's scalp itched worse than ever.

RAPUNZEL:	Doggone it, Mesmerelda. Why do you take so long to climb up my hair? Doug Toto climbs it as fast as a spider.
MESMERELDA:	Doug who? What are ya talkin' about?
RAPUNZEL:	Uh-oh! Never mind. Nothing.
MESMERELDA:	Whaddya mean—Nuttin'? Rapunzel, you got more hair dan brains. You want I should turn you into a giant mushroom dis time? Tell me about dis boyfriend of yours.
RAPUNZEL:	I knew I could never escape my prison if I were a giant mushroom, so I told her everything.
MESMERELDA:	So, dis guy, Doug Toto, is tryin' to break you out, eh? We'll see about dat!
N2:	Mesmerelda climbed back down Rapunzel's hair. When she reached the ground, she pulled out her magic pizza cutter and waved it at Rapunzel.
RAPUNZEL:	Oh dear, I feel so light-headed. *(touches head)* *Oh no!* My hair is gone! My scalp is absolutely hairless!
N1:	At the crack of dawn, Doug Toto showed up.
DOUG:	Rapunzel, Rapunzel, let down your hair!
N2:	Rapunzel stuck her head out the window.
DOUG:	Good grief, Rapunzel! You're bald as a bowling ball!
RAPUNZEL:	Well, doesn't *that* make me feel attractive?
DOUG:	I meant a very pretty bowling ball. Relax, Rapunzel. Your hair will grow back.
RAPUNZEL:	Not soon enough for you to climb up it and rescue me. Mesmerelda will be here soon with my bacon-and-eggs pizza.
DOUG:	Drat! I brought ropes to tie to the balcony so we could climb down together, but I was counting on using your hair to get myself up there.
RAPUNZEL:	Let's have some cold pizza and think of another plan. Here, catch!

Barbara McBride-Smith

DOUG:	Well, you didn't have to throw the whole box at me. Really, Rapunzel, littering is a bad habit. Look at all these pizza boxes you've thrown off your balcony. You must have been doing that for years. It's a real mess down here.
RAPUNZEL:	Hmmm, I think that mess of empty boxes is gonna help me solve my problem.
N1:	An hour later, Mesmerelda arrived at the apartment building and bounced up onto the balcony using her new jet-powered pogo stick.
N2:	But Doug and Rapunzel had already climbed down the stairway of pizza boxes he had built, and they were running down the street.
MESMERELDA:	I'll get you, my pretty! You and your little Doug Toto!
N1:	Mesmerelda jumped back on her pogo stick and bounced after them.
N2:	Boink! Boink!
RAPUNZEL:	Run faster, Doug! She's gaining on us!
N1:	Mesmerelda shifted her pogo stick into hyper-drive. But instead of going forward, she blasted upward until she was almost flying.
MESMERELDA:	Oh, no! Flying makes me sick. I tink I'm gonna throw up. *Helllllp!* I'm falling!
N2:	Mesmerelda lost her grip and plummeted down, hitting the street at a hundred miles an hour.
N1:	Along came a pizza delivery van and flattened what was left of her.
DAD:	Take that, you wicked old witch! Hello, Rapunzel dear. It's me— your dad. I'm no longer a pizza delivery van.
RAPUNZEL:	Way to go, Dad!
DAD:	Look, here comes your mother. She's no longer a pizza delivery van either. Mesmerelda's spell is broken.

MOM: Hello, everyone. It's wonderful to be human again. I hope I
            never see another pizza again as long as I live.

DAD: Me, either!

RAPUNZEL: My parents and I sold the pizza place to a guy named Hansel,
            and his sister, Gretel. They seemed to have a fondness for
            ovens. My hair never grew back, but I finally got to go to a real
            school.

DOUG: The same one I went to.

RAPUNZEL: And my new hairstyle made me the coolest girl in class. And
            the best thing was, I never again had to worry about having a
            bad hair day!

Get a Life, Cinder-Ella!

Based on the story "The Fairy Godmother's Assistant"
From a book by Bruce Lansky, *Girls to the Rescue**

Adapted for Story Theatre by Barbara McBride-Smith

Cast of three: NARRATOR (NARR) FAIRY GODMOTHER'S ASSISTANT (FGA)
ELLA

NARR: Ladies and gentlemen, it is my pleasure to introduce—the Fairy
          Godmother's Assistant!

FGA: Hi, that's me. The Fairy Godmother's Assistant. My job used to be
          quite simple really. And then, the Fairy Godmother announced
          that she was taking a vacation, and that I would have to sub for
          her while she was away. I was scared stiff! I didn't know any
          magic. I couldn't have turned a pumpkin into a coach if my life
          depended on it.

NARR: "Don't worry," the Fairy Godmother told her. "You're very
          sensible. I'm sure you'll find a way to handle whatever comes
          up. I'll only be gone for a couple of days."

FGA: To be honest with you, I didn't get much sleep that night. I kept
          wondering how I could possibly fill the Fairy Godmother's shoes.

NARR: The assistant got up early the next morning and went to the
          kitchen to make a pitcher of lemonade.

ELLA: *(knocks on door)* Yoo-hoo!

NARR: There was a knock at the door. The assistant opened it and
          there stood a young woman with a tear-stained face and
          wearing a tattered old dress.

FGA: Good morning! You must be looking for the Fairy Godmother.
          She's away on a little vacation. I'm her assistant, and I'll have
          her give you a call when she returns. Now, if you'll just leave
          me your name and your number…
          (FGA prepares to write. ELLA begins to cry softly)

* "The Fairy Godmother's Assistant." From *Girls to the Rescue* by Bruce Lansky.
(Meadowbrook Press, 1995). Adapted with permission from Meadowbrook Press,
5451 Smetana Drive, Minnetonka, MN 55343.

FGA: Oh my! I guess it can't wait. Uhhh, well, come in and have a glass of lemonade.

ELLA: Oh, thank you. *(cries louder, blows her nose)*

FGA: Here's a hanky, dear. Lemonade's coming right up. Now tell me what's bothering you.

ELLA: *(wipes her nose, sniffles, takes a deep breath)* My name is Ella, but my stepmother and stepsisters call me Cinder-Ella. You see, I'm always covered with cinders from cleaning the fireplace. They are so mean to me. They make me clean and cook and iron and sew and run errands. All they do is take naps and have fun and try to make themselves look beautiful. And now, I have to sew new gowns for them to wear to the king's royal ball. *(starts to cry again)* Oh, I want to go to the ball, too.

FGA: Mmmm. And I suppose you came here to ask the Fairy Godmother to get you to the ball. Is that it? *(ELLA nods yes)* I wish I could help you, dear. But I make lemonade, not magic.

ELLA: Can't you do *any*thing?

FGA: I'm afraid not. It's really up to *you*, Ella.

ELLA: *(drying her eyes)* Up to me?

FGA: Yes, it's quite simple. If you want to go to the ball...just go. And don't let anything or anyone stop you.

ELLA: But how can I go to the ball without an evening gown?

FGA: Don't look at me. You're the seamstress. If you can make gowns for your two stepsisters, why not make another one for yourself?

ELLA: But I can't afford to buy silk or velvet. How can I make a gown without any fabric?

FGA: Are there any velvet curtains in your house? Any silk bed sheets?

ELLA: *(smiling)* There sure are! But what about dancing slippers? I don't have any.

FGA: Then don't wear any.

ELLA: You mean I should go to the ball barefooted?

FGA: What choice do you have? Unless you want to wear those work
            boots you're wearing now. They're a good deal sturdier than
            glass slippers for dancing…and they won't fall off when you
            kick up your heels.

ELLA: But how am I supposed to get to the ball? The royal palace is
            almost a mile from my house.

FGA: I suppose you'll have to walk.

ELLA: That'll take quite a long time.

FGA: Start early.

ELLA: But they'll never let me in if I don't arrive in a fancy, horse-
            drawn carriage.

FGA: Probably not at the main gate. Hmmm, I don't suppose there
            will be anyone guarding the back door to the kitchen. Do you?

ELLA: I suppose not. But if the Prince asks me to dance, what should I
            say?

FGA: Ask him not to step on your boots. *(ELLA starts to laugh)*
            Cinder-Ella, go to the ball! What have you got to lose?

ELLA: Nothing! Nothing at all! Thank you. Thank you for all your
            help. I've got to run now. So many things to do!

FGA: There's something else, dear. Be home by midnight. Just a
            suggestion!

NARR: The next day around noon, there was a knock at the door.
            There stood Cinder-Ella, carrying a suitcase, and looking tired
            but happy.

FGA: Cinder-Ella! How was the ball?

ELLA: The ball was wonderful! The food, the music, the dancing!
            Everything was wonderful! And I got home before midnight. I
            just came by to say thanks again. I never would have gone
            without your help

FGA: Oh, I can't take any credit. You did it all yourself. By the way,
            what's in your suitcase?

ELLA: All my belongings. I really can't live with my stepmother and stepsisters any longer. So, I've decided to move into town and open up a dressmaker's shop. I'm a very good seamstress, you know. Well, thanks ever so much for your advice yesterday.

FGA: My pleasure, dear. May I be your first customer? When you're set up in town, I'll drop by for a new dress.

ELLA: Terrific! Shall I order you a matching pair of work boots? *(laughs)*

NARR: The Fairy Godmother returned a few days later. She didn't seem surprised about what had happened while she was away. She said, "I told you when I left that you could handle whatever came up."

FGA: I wonder if those were magic words.

Barbara McBride-Smith

Hershel and the Hanukkah Goblins

From the book by Eric Kimmel
Hershel and the Hanukkah Goblins *

Adapted for Story Theatre by Barbara McBride-Smith

Cast of ten:	NARRATOR 1 (N1)	GOBLIN 1
	NARRATOR 2 (N2)	GOBLIN 2
	HERSHEL	GOBLIN 3
	VILLAGER	KING OF GOBLINS (KING)
	RABBI	SOUND

N1: Long ago, on the first night of Hanukkah, a man named Hershel was walking down a road.

N2: He was tired and hungry, but he knew that when he reached the next village the people would be celebrating Hanukkah.

HERSHEL: There will be singing and dancing in every home. The candles in the menorahs will be twinkling. And the tables will be piled high with potato latkes. Mmmm, I can hardly wait!

N1: But when he arrived in that village, the houses were silent and dark. Not a single candle or potato latke was anywhere in sight.

HERSHEL: Hello! Anybody home? Isn't this the first night of Hanukkah? Why aren't you celebrating?

VILLAGER: We don't have Hanukkah in this village anymore.

HERSHEL: No Hanukkah? How can that be?

RABBI: It's because of the goblins. They haunt the old synagogue at the top of the hill. They hate Hanukkah.

VILLAGER: Whenever we try to light the menorah, the goblins blow out the candles. They break our children's dreidels. They throw our potato latkes on the floor.

RABBI: Those wicked goblins make our lives miserable all year long, but on Hanukkah, it's especially bad.

HERSHEL: I'm not afraid of goblins. Tell me how to get rid of them.

VILLAGER: It's not as easy as you might think.

RABBI: You must spend eight nights in the old synagogue. The Hanukkah candles must be lit each night. On the eighth night, the King of the Goblins must light all the candles himself.

HERSHEL: And that's the only way to break their power?

RABBI: Yes, I'm afraid so.

HERSHEL: Well, I'm not afraid. Surely I can outwit a few goblins. I'll do it!

VILLAGER: Good luck, Hershel! But you'll need food if you're going to stay up there for eight days.

RABBI: Here, take these hard-boiled eggs. You need them more than I do.

VILLAGER: I've got a jar of pickles. Let me get it for you.

RABBI: And, of course, you'll need to take this brass menorah and candles.

VILLAGER: Here's a box of matches. You might as well take this dreidel. No one here is using it.

RABBI: Good-bye Hershel, and thank you for trying to help us. I hope we'll see you again.

N2: To tell the truth, no one in the village really expected to see Hershel ever again. The goblins would surely destroy him, or at the very least, scare him away.

N1: It was long past sundown by the time Hershel reached the synagogue at the top of the hill. The old building was gloomy and dark. He opened the door.

SOUND: Creeeeek.

HERSHEL: Oooh, this feels like a place where goblins could live. Eight nights is a long time. Maybe I should just move on down the road to the next village. No, what am I saying? I promised to get rid of the goblins. Well, here goes—time to light the candles.

N2: Hershel put two candles in the menorah and set it on the windowsill. He struck a match and lit the *shammes* candle in the middle.

N1: He said the blessings and was about to light the other candle when he heard a voice.

GOBLIN 1:   *(high-pitched squeaky voice)* Hey! What are you doing!

N2:   A goblin had appeared out of nowhere and was hovering above Hershel. It was no bigger than a horsefly. It had a long, pointy tail and two little batwings.

HERSHEL: I'm lighting candles in this menorah. This is the first night of Hanukkah.

GOBLIN 1:   Oh no it's not! We don't allow Hanukkah around here.

HERSHEL: Is that so? And who's going to stop me? A little pipsqueak like you?

GOBLIN 1:   I may be little, but I'm verrrrry strong.

HERSHEL: Really? Can you crush rocks in your hand?

GOBLIN 1:   Crush rocks? You must be joking. Nobody's that strong!

HERSHEL: I am! Watch this.

N1:   Hershel took a hard-boiled egg from his pocket. In the dim light of the room, that egg looked just like a rock. Hershel squeezed the egg until the yolk and the white squished through his fingers.

HERSHEL: That's how hard I'm going to squeeze you if you try to stop me from lighting these candles.

GOBLIN 1:   *(fearfully)* You—you—you leave me alone.

HERSHEL: Gladly. If you let me light my candles in peace.

GOBLIN 1:   Well, all right. One night won't make any difference. But you better not be here tomorrow. Bigger and scarier goblins are coming. If they catch you lighting Hanukkah candles, you'll be sorry!

HERSHEL: *(to himself)* We'll see about that.

N2:   Hershel lit the first candle in the menorah.

N1:   On the second night, just as Hershel was finishing his dinner of pickles and hard-boiled eggs, another goblin appeared.

N2:   This one was big and fat and waddled like a goose.

HERSHEL: Hello. Would you like some pickles?

GOBLIN 2:   *(blubbery sounding voice)* Pickles? What are pickles?

HERSHEL: They're delicious to eat. Here, catch.

N1:   Hershel tossed the goblin a sour pickle. He caught it in his mouth.

GOBLIN 2:   *(gulp)* Mmmm! Pickles are good!

HERSHEL: Do you really like them? Well, I have plenty in this jar. Take all you want.

N2:   The greedy goblin grabbed as many pickles as his claws could hold, but when he tried to pull his fist out of the jar, he couldn't.

GOBLIN 2:   Oooo, I'm stuck! You put a spell on this jar. It won't let go of my hand!

HERSHEL: That's right. And it's a very powerful spell. I'm going to light these Hanukkah candles while you stand there with your hand in that jar and watch me. How do you like that?

GOBLIN 2:   No! No! No! I hate Hanukkah!

HERSHEL: Too bad. Get used to it. Here goes. I'm lighting the first candle.

N1:   Hershel lit the candles and sang all his favorite Hanukkah songs.

GOBLIN 2:   *(wailing and carrying on)* Arrrrrgh. Help! Help! Stop! Stop! Arrrrrgh!

HERSHEL: I'm finished celebrating Hanukkah for tonight. Now, shall I tell you how to break the spell on the pickle jar?

GOBLIN 2:   Yes! Yes! I can't stand it anymore!

HERSHEL: Just let go of the pickles. Your greed is the only thing holding you.

N2:   The goblin let go of the pickles, and his hand slipped out of the jar easily.

HERSHEL: Oooo, you're a bad man! You tricked me! You'll be sorry for this!

SOUND: *(shoe stomps floor)*

N1:   The furious goblin stamped his foot so hard that he shattered himself into a million pieces.

N2:   And the wind blew him away.

SOUND: Whoosh!

Barbara McBride-Smith

N1:	The third night came. As Hershel set the candles in the menorah, he felt something watching him. So instead of lighting the candles, he reached into his pocket, took out the dreidel, and began playing with it.
N2:	An hour passed. Hershel looked up. Sitting across the table from him was a huge goblin. It had a fiery red face and two enormous horns.
GOBLIN 3:	*(in a gruff voice)* When are you going to light the candles?
HERSHEL:	Later. There's plenty of time. This game is lots of fun.
GOBLIN 3:	What is that thing you're playing with? It looks like a top.
HERSHEL:	It's a dreidel. Don't you know about dreidels?
GOBLIN 3:	No.
HERSHEL:	Too bad. Dreidels are lots of fun. You can also make lots of money if you know how to play.
GOBLIN 3:	Really? I like money. I like lots of money. How do you play?
HERSHEL:	It's very simple. But you must have gold to begin the game. That's the first rule. Do you have gold?
GOBLIN 3:	Yes, I have gold. But I need more. Is this enough gold to begin the game?
N1:	The goblin poured a pile of gold coins onto the table.
HERSHEL:	Ah yes, that will do. Listen carefully now and look at the dreidel. This letter is *Shin.* *(NARRATOR 1 holds up sign showing this Hebrew letter)* If the dreidel lands with *Shin* facing up, you give me a handful of gold.
GOBLIN 3:	Okay. What about the other letters?
HERSHEL:	Well, this letter is *Hay.* *(NARRATOR 2 holds up sign showing this letter)* And if it comes up, you give me half your gold. Now, this letter is *Gimel.* *(NARRATOR 1 holds up sign)* If the dreidel lands on this letter, you give me all your gold. Understand?

GOBLIN 3:   Uhhh, yes, but there's one more letter. What happens with this one?

HERSHEL: Oh, that's *Nun*.
             (NARRATOR 2 holds up sign)
             If the letter *Nun* comes up, I don't have to give you anything.
             Ready to play the game? You get the first turn.

GOBLIN 3:   So now I get to spin the dreidel? Heh heh, here goes.
             (NARRATOR 1 holds up sign that says SHIN*)*

HERSHEL: Uh-oh, too bad. I'll take a handful of your gold. Why don't you
             try spinning again? Maybe you'll have better luck this time.

GOBLIN 3:   All right. I hope so. Here goes.
             (NARRATOR 2 holds up sign that says HAY*)*

HERSHEL: Oh what a shame. I must take half your gold. Tell you what—
             try one more time. Your luck is bound to improve.

GOBLIN 3:   Yeah, I'm trying hard. Here goes again.
             (NARRATOR 1 holds up sign that says GIMEL*)*

HERSHEL: Oh dear, this just isn't your night. Guess I'll have to take all your
             gold.

GOBLIN 3:   Ohhh, not fair! You take a turn spinning now.

HERSHEL: If you insist. Spin, dreidel, spin!
             (NARRATOR 2 holds up sign that says NUN*)*
             Oh my, look at that. It's *Nun*. I don't give you anything. I get to
             keep all the gold.

GOBLIN 3:   Grrrr.

HERSHEL: Wasn't that a fun game? Go get some more gold and we'll play
             again.

GOBLIN 3:   No! I don't want to play that game again. When are you going
             to light the Hanukkah candles?

HERSHEL: Oh, I'll do that later. There's plenty of time.

GOBLIN 3:   Not for me. I'm leaving now. I don't like your game. I don't like
             Hanukkah. And I don't like *you!*

HERSHEL: Oh, please don't go. I know lots of other games. Stay awhile.
             We'll have fun.

GOBLIN 3:	No, we won't! Good-bye!
N2:	The goblin spread his wings, swooped out the door, and flew off into the night.
N1:	Hershel lit the Hanukkah candles all by himself.
N2:	On the following nights, other goblins came.
N1:	One had six heads.
N2:	One had three eyes.
N1:	All were terrible and fierce.
N2:	They growled and roared and changed themselves into horrible shapes.
N1:	They tried to stop Hershel from lighting the Hanukkah candles. But Hershel fooled them all.
N2:	Finally, the seventh night arrived. Hershel lit the *shammes* candle. Then he lit seven more candles in the menorah. He sat back to enjoy the light.
N1:	Where were the goblins? Had they finally given up?
N2:	Hershel felt very sleepy. *(HERSHEL yawns)* His eyes closed.
N1:	Suddenly he sat up. He heard a horrible sound. It was a voice, coming from far away.
KING:	Happy Hanukkah, Hershel!
HERSHEL:	Who is that? Who's there?
KING:	Don't you know who I am, Hershel? Weren't you expecting me? I am the King of the Goblins!!
SOUND:	*Crash! (cymbals)*
N2:	The voice shattered the windows of the synagogue.
N1:	The candles flickered but they did not go out.
HERSHEL:	You're too early! You're not supposed to come until tomorrow!

KING: Don't worry, Hershel. I am far away tonight. Enjoy this Hanukkah evening, my friend. It will be your last. *(laughs)* Tomorrow night I will come for you. You can't fool me like you fooled those slave goblins of mine. *(laughter fades into distance)*

HERSHEL: Ohhh, what am I going to do? The King of the Goblins is on his way, and I have no power to stop him. Unless…unless… Hmmm. It's a big chance, but I'll have to take it.

N2:   Sure enough, the last night of Hanukkah came. Hershel set the candles in the menorah. But instead of placing it on the windowsill, he put the menorah and the box of matches on a small table near the door.

N1:   Then he sat down to wait.

N2:   Suddenly the whole synagogue began to shake. A gust of wind ripped the door from its hinges.

SOUND: *(blowing wind and crashing cymbals)*

KING: Hershel! Hershel, are you still here?!

HERSHEL: Did I hear something?

KING: It is I, the King of the Goblins!

HERSHEL: *(laughs)* Oh, don't be silly. You're one of the boys from the village acting silly. You're trying to scare me, aren't you?

KING: I am not a boy! I am the King of the Goblins.

HERSHEL: I'll believe it when I see it. Show yourself to me.

N1:   The goblin king stepped into the doorway of the synagogue.

KING: Behold! I stand before you. I *am* the King of the Goblins. Do you believe me now?

N2:   Hershel tried not to look, but even in the darkness he could see the outline of a monstrous shape filling the doorway.

HERSHEL: *(pretending not to see the KING)* No, it's too dark. I can't see anything. But I think there's a candlestick and some matches by the doorway. I can't see them myself, but perhaps you can find them. If you light a few candles, then I can see who you really are.

Barbara McBride-Smith

KING:	Indeed you shall!
N1:	The King of the Goblins didn't figure out that Hershel was playing a trick on him.
N2:	The king struck a match and lit the *shammes* candle.
HERSHEL:	Oh dear, I'm sorry to say that's not nearly enough light to see who you are. It's still too dark. There are plenty of candles there. Why not light them all?
KING:	Yes, why not?!
N1:	The hideous goblin took the *shammes* candle and lit the others one by one.
N2:	Hershel's eyes grew wider and wider as each candle caught the flame.
HERSHEL:	Two, three, four. Oh yes, I can see you a little better now. But I'm still not sure if you're only a village boy playing a trick on me.
N1:	The goblin continued to light the candles.
HERSHEL:	Five, six, seven…
KING:	Look closely. Now do you believe that I am the King of the Goblins?
HERSHEL:	I can almost see you. But I can't be sure that you're not a silly village boy. Just a bit more light. One more candle ought to do it.
KING:	There! All the candles on this table are burning brightly. Now, Hershel, do you know who I am?
HERSHEL:	I know you're not Queen Esther.
KING:	Very funny! Enjoy the joke! It will be your last!!
HERSHEL:	That's what you think. Be gone from here, or I'll take a stick to you.
KING:	How dare you speak to the King of the Goblins that way!!
HERSHEL:	I'll speak to you any way I please. You have no power now. Your spell is broken. Look beside you. Those candles aren't ordinary candles. They're Hanukkah candles, and you lit every one of them yourself!

KING: Rawrrrrrrrr!

N2: The King of the Goblins was furious. As he roared, the earth trembled and a mighty wind arose.

SOUND: *(wind blows)*

N1: The wind ripped off the synagogue roof and blew down the walls.

N2: But the menorah was not destroyed. The candles never flickered.

N1: And then the wind vanished as suddenly as it had risen.

HERSHEL: Wha—wha—what happened? Well, look at that! The menorah is still here, right where I put it. The spirit of Hanukkah has triumphed over the goblins. I'd better hurry back to the village. I don't want to miss the celebration.

N2: As Hershel walked down the hill, he saw a menorah in every window of the village. The candles were gleaming, lighting his way into the village.

VILLAGER
 & RABBI: *(clapping)* Hurraaaay, Hershel! Our hero!

VILLAGER: Thank you, Hershel. You got rid of the goblins!

RABBI: You're a brave man, Hershel. We'll always remember you when we celebrate Hanukkah.

N1: And every year after that, the little village had a grand celebration at Hanukkah.

N2: And they would always say...

VILLAGER: Remember the time that brave man Hershel tricked the goblins and saved Hanukkah?

Santaberry and the Snard

From the book by Alice and Joel Schick
*Santaberry and the Snard**

Adapted for Story Theatre by Barbara McBride-Smith

Cast of six:

NARRATOR 1 (N1)		SNARD
NARRATOR 2 (N2)		ELF
SANTA		MRS. CLAUS (MRS. C)

N1: Far, far away, in the icy wastes of the North Pole, there live some creatures called Snards. They are large and furry, with very long claws.

N2: Snards are gentle beasts. They use their claws only to dig in the snow for Arctic strawberries.

N1: Life is hard for Snards. They are very big, and Arctic strawberries are very small. So Snards spend almost all their time looking for food.

N2: Few people have ever seen a Snard, and most people don't believe they are real.

N1: There was a time when even Santa Claus didn't believe in Snards.

N2: His elves told him that they had actually seen them.

ELF: It's true, Santa! We've seen those big, old hairy Snards roaming around in the ice fields not far from here.

SANTA: Snards! Ho, ho, ho! Stuff and nonsense!

N1: But one year a peculiar thing happened. It was December twenty-third. Christmas was coming fast.

N2: Santa and his elves worked late into the night. The toys had to be ready, and they had to be perfect.

N1: Most nights, Santa fed his reindeer at six o'clock, but tonight he was so busy he forgot.

---

* *Santaberry and the Snard* by Alice and Joel Schick. (Lippincott, 1976, 1979). Adapted with permission of Alice and Joel Schick, P.O. Box 101, Monterey, MA 01245. The authors note that, although the original book is out of print, they have copies available for sale and autographing.

SANTA:	Uh-oh.
N2:	Those hungry reindeer were out in the barn snorting and stamping their feet. They wanted their supper, and they wanted it two hours ago.
SANTA:	I'm coming! I'm coming!
N1:	Santa hurried out to the barn, wearing his red longjohns. He didn't even stop for a coat or a hat.
N2:	He fed the reindeer. He talked to them gently and stroked their soft, velvety noses. Santa stayed out in the barn a long time.
N1:	Meanwhile, a huge Snard was headed toward Santa's village. It was late, but the poor beast was still hunting.
N2:	His eyesight was very bad, so he had a lot of trouble finding food. He had found only four strawberries all day. His great belly ached with hunger.
SNARD:	Oooh, I am sooo hungry.
N1:	Santa said good night to the reindeer, closed the barn door, and walked out into the snowy darkness.
SANTA:	Well, look at that. The lights are off in the workshop. The elves must have finished all the toys and gone to bed. Guess I'll turn in for the night, too.
N1:	Just then, the nearsighted Snard came up behind Santa.
SNARD:	Wow!! That's the biggest strawberry I've ever seen!
N2:	In a flash, the Snard popped Santa into his mouth and swallowed him.
SNARD:	Yum-yum!
N1:	At last, the Snard felt full. He curled up behind the barn and went to sleep.
SNARD:	ZZZZZZ! *(loud snoring noise)*
N2:	Back at the house, Mrs. Claus was worried about Santa.
MRS. C:	Oh, my! Look how late it is. Surely Santa has finished in the workshop by now. He needs his supper and a good night's sleep.

Barbara McBride-Smith

N1:	At midnight, Mrs. Claus went out to the workshop. She asked the elves…
MRS. C:	Have you seen Santa?
ELF:	He went out to feed the reindeer hours ago.
N2:	Mrs. Claus went to the barn.
N1:	The reindeer were sleeping quietly, but Santa wasn't there.
N2:	The next morning Santa was still missing.
MRS. C:	Now, where could he be? It's Christmas Eve. If he doesn't get back here soon, he won't have time to get everything ready for his journey. Come on, elves. Let's pack the sleigh for Santa.
N1:	By five o'clock, the sleigh was ready to go.
ELF:	We'll hitch up the reindeer, Mrs. C.
MRS. C:	I'll make sandwiches for Santa to take along with him. He's going to be mighty hungry!
N2:	By nine o'clock that night Santa still wasn't home.
MRS. C:	Goodness, gracious! Where is that dear old man?
N1:	Meanwhile, behind the barn, the Snard woke up. He didn't feel well at all. That large strawberry he had eaten was pounding on his stomach from the inside.
SNARD:	This is terrible! This feels worse than feeling hungry! *Burrrrrp!*
N2:	Up came that big strawberry, waving its arms and shouting.
SANTA:	Arrrrgh! Let me outta here!
N1:	The Snard squinted at that strange berry.
SNARD:	Why, you're not a strawberry!!
SANTA:	Of course I'm not a strawberry, you silly goose! I'm Santa Claus!!
SNARD:	Well, I'm not a goose, I'm a Snard.
SANTA:	Phooey!
N2:	Santa ran to the house, where he found Mrs. Claus, frantic with worry.

SANTA:	You'll never believe it, Mrs. Claus. I was swallowed by a Snard! He mistook me for a strawberry.
MRS. C:	I'll be doggoned! So there really are Snards!
ELF:	Santa, look how late it is. You'll never get all these presents delivered by morning.
SANTA:	Oh, dear. Oh, dear.
MRS. C:	Wait just a minute. I have an idea. Where's that Snard?
N1	The Snard was still behind the barn, thinking about that strange strawberry he had burped up.
SNARD:	I could have sworn it was a strawberry.
MRS. C:	Come on, Snard! You made all this trouble. Now you're going to help get us out of it.
N2:	She dragged the Snard to the front of the sleigh.
MRS. C:	Hitch him up, Santa. I'll be right back.
N1:	In a few minutes, Mrs. Claus came back with a huge pair of wings.
MRS. C:	Put these on, Snard! Now look, Santa. You'll have to fly extra fast tonight. This Snard will give you a lot more power up front.
SANTA:	Okey, dokey. I'll give it a try.
N2:	Santa climbed up into the sleigh and cracked his whip.
SANTA:	Giddy-up, Snard!
ELF:	Good-bye, Santa! Good luck!
N1:	Off they went—Santa, the sleigh full of presents, the eight reindeer, and the Snard.
N2:	And all the presents were delivered on time that Christmas Eve.
N1:	Santa was pleased.
SANTA:	Whew. Thank goodness we made it in time.
N2:	Mrs. Claus was pleased.

Barbara McBride-Smith

MRS. C:	*(clapping hands)* Very good, very good.
N1:	The elves were pleased.
ELF:	Yipppeee!
N2:	But no one was more pleased than the Snard.
SNARD:	Oh boy, oh boy!
SANTA:	Snard, I officially declare you an honorary reindeer.
MRS. C:	And you're invited over for strawberry upside-down cake every Sunday.
SNARD:	Oh boy, oh boy, oh boy!
N1:	And sure enough, every Sunday after that, the Snard came to dinner and feasted on two dozen strawberry upside-down cakes.
SNARD:	Yum-yum!
ELF:	And that's how Santa Claus came to believe in Snards.

Twelfth Night

A Play by William Shakespeare

Scripted for Story Theatre by Barbara McBride-Smith

Cast of thirteen:
NARRATOR 1 (N1)	CAPTAIN
NARRATOR 2 (N2)	SIR TOBY
ORSINO	SIR ANDREW
OLIVIA	MARIA
MALVOLIO	FESTE
SEBASTIAN	ANTONIO
VIOLA-CESARIO	

N1: This is the story of a shipwreck.

N2: It is also a story of mistaken identities and true love.

ORSINO: Yes, love sweet love! But the lady does not return my love. Oh, woe is me!

N1: The story begins in a country called Illyria next to the Adriatic Sea.

N2: Illyria was ruled by a young duke named Orsino. He lived in a beautiful palace not far from the shore.

N1: He was tall, good-looking, and very rich. He had everything he could possibly want...except for one thing.

ORSINO: Olivia! I am in love with Olivia, but she refuses even to look at me. She says she is in mourning for her brother and father who became ill and died very suddenly. How long will her sorrow last?

OLIVIA: My sorrow will never end, and I will never marry. If any man comes to my door, I will send him away. Oh, woe is me!

ORSINO: *(pantomimes writing a letter)* Dear Olivia, I beg of you. Please allow me to come for a visit. I long to gaze upon your face and hear your voice.

OLIVIA: *(pantomimes reading letter)* Malvolio! Please throw this letter away. And if Orsino sends more chocolates or flowers or jewelry, send them back.

MALVOLIO: Yes, my lady. And if one of his servants darkens your door again, I'll give him a swift kick in the seat of his pants.

OLIVIA: That's not necessary, Malvolio. Be polite, but turn him away. I wish to be alone in my sorrow.

N2: Malvolio was Olivia's butler.

N1: His name, Malvolio, is an Italian word that means: "I don't like you very much, and I hope you have lousy luck!"

N2: He was as ugly as Orsino was handsome. He was shaped like a pear, and his legs looked like matchsticks. He was rude to everyone and terribly stuck-up.

N1: Malvolio was twice Olivia's age, and not at all her type, but he was secretly in love with her.

MALVOLIO: Someday Olivia will see what a fine catch I am, and she will beg me to marry her.

N2: Meanwhile, in another seaside town called Montegolfo, there lived a pair of twins. *(SEBASTIAN wears a backward baseball cap; VIOLA wears a bonnet)*

N1: They looked like identical twins, except for one thing. One of them was a boy, and the other was a girl.

N2: But other than that, you couldn't tell them apart. They were the same height, wore the same short haircut, and even sounded alike.

VIOLA: Sebastian, let's ask Mother if we can go for a boat ride along the coast today.

SEBASTIAN: But, Viola, we don't have a boat.

VIOLA: I know that, my silly brother. I've made friends with the captain of that small fishing boat at the dock. He agreed to take us along today. We'll be back before dark.

N1: The twins' mother agreed to let them go, so they packed their lunch and set sail with the captain and his crew.

SEBASTIAN: What a glorious day, Viola! How would I ever manage to entertain myself without you and your clever ideas?

Barbara McBride-Smith

N2:	Then suddenly, without warning, a storm came up, and the ship began to buck like a wild horse.
N1:	A gigantic wave tossed the little ship into the air. It came down with a crash and split apart.
SEBASTIAN:	Viola!! Where are you? Are you all right?
VIOLA:	Sebastian!! I'm alive. Swim, brother! Swim as hard as you can. We'll find land, I'm sure of it!
N2:	Both Viola and Sebastian were excellent swimmers, but the storm was so fierce they were almost drowned.
N1:	Luckily, Sebastian found a piece of the boat's wooden mast and was able to grab hold of it.
N2:	The last Viola saw of her brother, he was holding to that piece of mast as if it were his only hope for survival.
N1:	Viola!! There's room for you. Climb on!
VIOLA:	I'm trying, Sebastian, but I can't reach you. Help!!
N2:	A monstrous wave picked up Viola, heaved her ashore, and left her unconscious on the beach.
CAPTAIN:	My lady, wake up. We're alive. Remember me? I'm the captain of the fishing boat. We survived a terrible tempest.
VIOLA:	But where are the others? My brother! Where's Sebastian?
CAPTAIN:	I don't know, my lady. But he's a strong young man. He probably washed ashore somewhere. Don't worry. He's sure to turn up sooner or later.
VIOLA:	Of course. He's alive and well. I know I'll find him. Sooner or later.
CAPTAIN:	Now come with me, my lady. I know this country. It's called Illyria. Very friendly. We'll find dry clothes and food, and then we'll go to the duke's palace and introduce ourselves.
VIOLA:	Do you suppose the duke will help me find my brother?
CAPTAIN:	Oh, my lady Viola. Duke Orsino has troubles of his own. He is lovesick for a young woman named Olivia, but she ignores him. He is able to think of nothing else.

VIOLA: Hmmm. Perhaps if I help the duke, he will help me. I have an idea, Captain. Take me to a shop where I can find clothes. Men's clothes…in my size.

N1: The captain took Viola to a tailor where she bargained for a suit of clothes. When she came out of the shop, she looked exactly like a young man. *(VIOLA puts on a backward baseball cap)*

CAPTAIN: Odds bodikins, my lady! You are the spittin' image of your brother! But why have you chosen to dress this way?

VIOLA: I will go to the duke and ask for a job as his page. When he sees what a faithful servant I can be, he will use his power to help me find my brother, Sebastian.

CAPTAIN: So, you are no longer Miss Viola?

VIOLA: No, Captain. For a while I will be…Cesario! Yes, that's it. Cesario. That's a good name for Duke Orsino's newest page, isn't it? Wish me luck.

CAPTAIN: Good luck, Miss…uh, Mister. Yes, of course, good luck, Cesario!

N2: Sure enough, Viola—who was now Cesario—got a job as Duke Orsino's page.

N1: And before long, she had won the duke's trust, and Orsino was telling her of his love for Olivia.

ORSINO: Oh, Cesario, what shall I do? Olivia throws away my letters. She returns my gifts without even untying the ribbons. Oh, woe is me.

VIOLA-CESARIO: Sir, I happen to know a great deal about girls. I…er…I come from a family with many sisters. Perhaps I could talk to Olivia for you. Maybe I could soften her heart.

ORSINO: I'm willing to try anything. Oh, thank you, Cesario! Go at once to Olivia's house. But watch out for her butler. He's a nasty fellow.

N2: Now, you must remember that although Viola was dressed as a young man and had taken a young man's name, she was still very much a girl underneath her disguise.

N1: And during the time she had been working for Orsino, she had fallen in love with him! Now it was her duty to persuade Olivia to love the very same man she herself loved.

N2: What a mix-up!

VIOLA-CESARIO: I didn't expect this to happen. But I must be a good servant and do as I promised. I'm off to see Olivia.

SOUND: *(doorbell rings)*

MALVOLIO: Who are *you?* And whaddya want? If you're selling stuff, we don't need any!

VIOLA-CESARIO: My name is Cesario. My master, the duke, has sent me to deliver a message to the good lady Olivia.

MALVOLIO: So, what's the message?

VIOLA-CESARIO: It is a private matter, sir. I must speak with her personally.

MALVOLIO: Impossible! Miss Olivia has eyes and ears only for *me!* Now turn your skinny self around and run away from this door as fast as you can, or I'll give you a good swift kick with my shiny boot!

OLIVIA: Malvolio! What are you doing? I have never seen this young man before, but he seems terribly sincere. Let him in. I will speak with him.

MALVOLIO: Oh please, my lady. He's nothing but a pest. Let me get rid of him for you.

OLIVIA: No, Malvolio. I like his looks. He will stay and tell me his message. *You* will go! Quickly.

VIOLA-CESARIO: Thank you, my lady Olivia. I have come to tell you of my master's love for you. He is a good man and wishes to marry you. Please don't be cruel and keep your heart from him. He will be the most wonderful husband in the world. Why, I would happily marry him myself...uh, *if* I were a woman, that is!

OLIVIA: What a good man *you* are to speak so well for your master. I can see why he trusts you. Please stay and have tea, and we will talk more.

N1: Do you have any idea what's happening here? Olivia is falling in love with Cesario, who is really Viola, of course.

N2: That's how true love happens. You can't control it. It takes you by surprise.

N1: Egads, this is confusing! Viola, pretending to be a man, is pleading with Olivia to marry Orsino, when all the time Viola is in love with Orsino herself.

N2: And at the very same time, Olivia, who was determined to stay unmarried her whole life, has fallen in love with Cesario, who is really Viola in disguise.

N1: It couldn't get any worse.

N2: Yes, I'm afraid it could.

N1: As soon as Cesario—otherwise known as Viola—had left that afternoon, Olivia was desperate to see him again. How could she let him know that she'd like for him to visit the next day?

OLIVIA: Oh, I have a splendid idea! Why, look at this. *(bends over and pretends to pick up something from floor)* It's a ring! That nice young man must have dropped his ring. Malvolio, hurry after him. Give him his ring and tell him that he is welcome to visit me again tomorrow.

MALVOLIO: But, my lady, I don't run very well. Just let him return home, and I will send the ring to him tomorrow.

OLIVIA: Oh, my dear sweet Malvolio. You *do* want to make me happy, don't you?

MALVOLIO: Of course I do, Miss Olivia.

OLIVIA: Then *run*. Quickly!

N2: Malvolio took off running down the road after Cesario…

N1: Who was really Viola, of course.

N2: And when Malvolio caught up with Cesario…

N1: Viola, that is…

N2: That pear-shaped butler was huffing and puffing like the big bad wolf.

MALVOLIO: *(puffing)* Stop! Hey there! Stop! My mistress sends you this ring you dropped on her floor.

VIOLA-CESARIO: Ring? But I didn't have a ring...or did I? Oh yes, *that* ring! She wants to return my ring, does she? Hmmm. I think I understand.

N1: Yes, Viola did understand. Olivia had sent her very own ring as a secret message. Olivia had fallen in love with her.

N2: With Cesario, that is.

VIOLA-CESARIO: Oh, what a pickle I'm in now!

N1: Meanwhile, back at Olivia's house, there are some other characters in this story that you must meet.

N2: First, there's Olivia's uncle.

SIR TOBY: Cheerio! I am Sir Toby Belch. As you can see by the size of my belly, I love eating and drinking and having a good time. There's nothing more fun than playing a clever practical joke on somebody who deserves it.

N1: Next, there's Sir Toby's young friend, who came to visit Sir Toby at Olivia's house, and became a sort of fixture in the place.

SIR ANDREW: I beg your pardon! A fixture, indeed! I remain here because I am hopelessly in love with Olivia, and I am sure that someday she will love me in return. And then we will be married and live happily ever. My name is Sir Andrew Aguecheek.

N2: Thank you, Sir Andrew. And now let us meet Feste.

FESTE: Hello, hello, hello! I'm Feste, Olivia's jester. You know, the castle comedian. Listen to this: Knock-knock!

SIR TOBY: Who's there?

FESTE: Ach.

SIR TOBY: Ach who?

FESTE: Gesundheit!

SIR TOBY: *(laughing)* Ah, Feste. You're a barrel of laughs. Go on, do another one.

FESTE: Knock-knock.

SIR ANDREW: Who's there?

FESTE:	Yah.
SIR ANDREW:	Yah who?
FESTE:	Ride 'em, cowboy!
SIR T & SIR A:	*(both laughing and clapping)* Bravo! Bravo!
SIR TOBY:	Maria! Bring more cider. Our mugs are dry! And please join us, my dear, in a toast to Feste. Funniest man in Illyria. Cheers!
N1:	Maria was Olivia's maid.
MARIA:	Oh, I'm not just the maid, my dear. I'm also the cook, the seamstress, and Miss Olivia's personal secretary. She simply couldn't run this house without me.
SIR TOBY:	Be careful, Maria. You're getting as stuck-up as Malvolio.
MARIA:	Oh, please no, Sir Toby. *(laughing)* I could never get my nose as high into the air as Malvolio can poke his. A rare piece of work he is!
FESTE:	Indeed! And here's the best joke of all. He thinks Miss Olivia fancies him. He's sure she'll marry him someday.
SIR ANDREW:	Not a chance! Miss Olivia is going to marry me!
SIR TOBY:	How true, how true, Sir Andrew. And when Olivia marries you, you will become my very own nephew-in-law. Let's have another glass of cider in your honor, good sir.
MARIA:	Fellas! I've just had a delicious idea! Let's play a little joke on Malvolio. I'll write a letter to the chump, imitating Miss Olivia's handwriting. I'll tell him that a certain someone admires him so very much, especially when he smiles and wears his brightest yellow stockings on his shapely legs.
FESTE:	Jolly good fun, Maria! You write the letter, and I'll slip it under his bedroom door. What a fool he'll make of himself.
MARIA:	Serves him right. He's always breaking up our parties and telling us how lazy we are.
SIR ANDREW:	Not to mention how he's always acting like a goody-two-shoes to impress Miss Olivia.

Barbara McBride-Smith

N2: So that night, Maria wrote the note to Malvolio.

MARIA: *(pantomimes writing)* Dearest Malvolio. Your sweet smile warms my heart. And when you wear your gorgeous yellow stockings, the sight of your legs nearly takes my breath away. How lucky I would be to marry so handsome a gentleman. Love, Your Secret Admirer.

N1: Feste slipped the note under Malvolio's door.

N2: The next morning Malvolio came waltzing into Miss Olivia's breakfast room grinning like an idiot and wearing the brightest canary-colored stockings you have ever seen.

MALVOLIO: Good morning, Olivia dear. *(blows a kiss at her)* You must find me unbelievably attractive today.

OLIVIA: Oh, you're unbelievable all right, Malvolio. Please go to your room and lock the door. And don't come out again until you're ready to behave yourself!

MALVOLIO: But Olivia, you said you admired my legs. You even signed the letter with "Love." I was certain you were ready to marry me.

OLIVIA: Letter? What letter? And as for marrying you, you really have gone off your rocker. The only man I want to marry is Cesario.

SIR ANDREW: *(holding his hand to his ear as though listening through a wall)* Cesario! She wants to marry Cesario! No! She is supposed to marry me! I'll teach that little whippersnapper page a lesson. I'll challenge him to a sword fight.

SIR TOBY: Uh-oh. This could get dangerous. Hmmm. I think I know how to prevent things from becoming bloody.

N1: Sir Toby sent the official fighting swords to the blacksmith and got him to grind off the points and sharp edges.

N2: The time and place for the sword fight were arranged.

VIOLA-CESARIO: I can't believe he wants to fight me to win the love of Olivia. Sometimes men can be so blind! And I have never even held a sword. I don't believe in fighting. But if I don't show up, I'll be called a coward and thrown in jail...or worse.

SIR ANDREW:	Whatever got into me? Challenging someone to a sword fight! I must be crazy. I know absolutely nothing about fighting. I know even less about swords.
N1:	It was really a very funny scene that day as Cesario…
N2:	who was really Viola, of course…
N1:	and Sir Andrew stood facing each other…
N2:	holding blunt swords and shaking with fear.
N1:	Before either of them could strike a blow, a very large man with a black beard ran out from behind a tree and knocked their swords out of their hands.
ANTONIO:	Stop that, both of you! You're too young to play with such dangerous toys!
SIR TOBY:	Who are you? And who invited you to this private duel?
ANTONIO:	I am Antonio. I have already saved this young man once, so now I must save him again!
N2:	So, who was this large bearded man named Antonio?
VIOLA-CESARIO:	Yes, who are you? Have we met before?
N1:	If you thought this story was already complicated enough, just wait until you hear this part. This is what happened earlier that day.
N2:	Pay attention, everybody. You could get lost in this plot!
N1:	Remember when we last saw Viola's twin brother, Sebastian, hanging onto a chunk of wood in the ocean and trying not to drown?
N2:	Well, Sebastian didn't drown. He was rescued by the captain of a pirate ship. His name was Antonio.
ANTONIO:	Unfortunately, I am also an old enemy of Duke Orsino's. I must stay out of sight or get arrested. Here, Sebastian, take some money and find us a place to stay.
SEBASTIAN:	Thank you, Antonio, my friend. I'll find lodging, and then I'll search for my sister Viola. Where shall we meet?

ANTONIO: There's a park at the edge of town.

N1: It was the very same park where the sword fight was about to take place.

N2: Antonio got there first.

N1: And when he saw his young friend, Sebastian...

N2: who was really Viola, of course...

N1: facing Sir Andrew in a sword fight, he put a stop to it.

N2: The duke's guards, who had been following Antonio the pirate, captured him and took him off to jail.

VIOLA-CESARIO: Whew! I don't know who that big fella was, but I'm glad he saved my life. I think it's time for me to get back to the duke's palace.

N1: No sooner was Cesario...

N2: who was really Viola...

N1: out of sight, than who should come walking into the park to meet Antonio the pirate?

N2: Sebastian?

N1: Yes, of course. Sebastian!

SIR ANDREW: I thought you had run away, you coward! So you want to fight some more, do you? Then pick up your sword, and we'll get on with it.

SEBASTIAN: Who me? But why would I want to fight you? I don't even know you.

OLIVIA: What's all this noise about? I could hear it all the way from the house? Sir Andrew, why are you holding that sword? Uncle Toby, did you arrange this silly game? Oh, my darling Cesario, you could have been hurt. Come to the house with me, and I'll make you some tea.

SEBASTIAN: Are you talking to me?

OLIVIA: Of course, my love. After you have rested, we must talk.

SEBASTIAN:	Tea and talk. Of course, my lady. Whatever you say.
N2:	After Olivia and Cesario…
N1:	who was really Sebastian, of course…
N2:	had tea, she said to him:
OLIVIA:	Cesario, I see a great change in how you look at me. If you love me as I think, shall we be married at once?
N1:	He wasn't Cesario. He was Sebastian! But he had fallen in love with Olivia the moment he laid eyes on her. All he could say was:
SEBASTIAN:	Yes! Send for the priest!
N2:	The priest arrived, and in a very few minutes…
OLIVIA:	I do.
SEBASTIAN:	I do.
N1:	…the wedding was over.
N2:	Suddenly, Sebastian remembered his promise to meet his friend, Antonio the pirate. He went running out to the park to find him and explain what happened.
N1:	Meanwhile, Cesario…
VIOLA-CESARIO:	I'm really Viola, of course.
N2:	…was happy to have escaped the sword fight. She went home to Orsino and was trying to explain what happened.
N1:	It was at that moment that the duke's guards came crashing into the palace with their prisoner, Antonio the pirate.
VIOLA-CESARIO:	That's the man who stopped the sword fight! He saved me!
ANTONIO:	Yes, and it wasn't the first time I saved you. You'd have drowned if I hadn't rescued you from the ocean, Sebastian.
VIOLA-CESARIO:	Sebastian? You know my brother Sebastian? You have seen him alive and well? I must find him!
N2:	A short time later, on one of the tiny side streets of town, Viola and Sebastian found each other.

VIOLA:	Sebastian, my dear brother! You're alive!
SEBASTIAN:	And so are you, sweet Viola. Oh, I was afraid you had been drowned at sea. I'm so happy to see you. But why are you dressed as a boy?
VIOLA:	It's a long story.
N1:	Indeed, it has been.
N2:	But it ends well.
N1:	Duke Orsino asked Viola to marry him.
VIOLA:	I do.
ORSINO:	I do.
N2:	Olivia and Sebastian were reunited. *(they clasp hands and sigh "Ahh")*
N1:	Antonio the pirate was pardoned and became a good citizen of Illyria.
ANTONIO:	I think I'll run for governor.
MALVOLIO:	As for me, I—Malvolio the Magnificent—am leaving this place and never coming back!
SIR:	And I—Sir Andrew the Amazing—am leaving with you!
MARIA:	Good riddance!
N2:	That evening, Maria and Sir Toby and Feste had a lovely celebration.
N1:	They talked late into the night of how a terrible shipwreck had brought to Illyria's shores a most confusing story...
N2:	of mistaken identities and true love.
FESTE:	At least I am paid to play the fool. The rest of the world does it for nothing!

Tips for Writing Your Own Scripts

Now that you've worked with the scripts in this book, you're ready to create some of your own. The more you do it, the easier it gets. Trite, but true. You, the teacher/director working alone, can script a story in an hour or less. Or you can give your students the valuable experience of scripting a story together. Even though it takes longer, I'm an advocate of team scripting. To get you started, here are a few suggestions based on my in-the-trenches experience over the years. I've learned more from my mistakes than I have from my victories, so don't be discouraged if your first script isn't a masterpiece. In any case, remember: When working with kids, the process is more important than the product.

Choosing Material

Almost any story can be scripted for Story Theatre, but some transpose more easily than others. The first thing to look for as you scan the print version is dialogue—lots of it. The more of those quotation marks you see, the fewer speaking lines you'll have to create from scratch. The next thing to check is the number of characters. Most of my scripts have at least four character parts plus narrators. The variety of voices and the interaction of several characters make the story more interesting to the audience. Avoid stories that require a great deal of physical action or long explanatory passages to clarify the plot. As much as possible, the plot should be revealed through the characters' lines.

For your first attempt, begin with a fable. A well-written fable is short, the characters are lively, the plot is clear, descriptive passages are minimized, and the ending is succinct. When I teach scripting to my students, beginning in second or third grade, I use a collection of Aesop's fables or Arnold Lobel's award-winning *Fables* (Harper & Row, 1980).

Once you get a handle on the basics of scripting, you can move on to more challenging material. Picture books adapt with moderate effort, unless the story depends heavily on the illustrations. Harry Allard's books about The Stupid Family, for example, are wonderful read-alouds, but they don't transpose easily to Story Theatre—too many sight gags. Allard's Miss Nelson books, on the other hand, can be converted to performance with some painless transformation of narrative to dialogue and the use of simple costumes.

I particularly enjoy working with picture book versions of folktales, both traditional and contemporary in style. Eric Kimmel, a former professor of children's literature and a fine oral teller in his own right, writes his folktale books in a style that practically jumps off the page and speaks for itself. I am always on the lookout for picture books with this definitive "voice"—dialogue and narration written with the full force of a culture behind it. If the story already has anachronisms, idioms, colloquialisms, double-entendre, and opportunities for verbal shtick, my work as a scriptwriter is as easy as falling off a log. If the story is written in what I call a "stained-glass voice," the effort to transpose it to an interesting performance piece is more labor intensive.

Narrative poetry is usually easy to script on paper, but difficult to perform effectively. Students can lapse into a singsong rhythmical pattern and lose the meaning of the story. More interesting, perhaps, is creating your own poetic version of a familiar story. You see an example of this in my "Three Billy Goats Gruff," which I constructed with the help of a third grade class. Whenever possible, use refrains that can be repeated by the whole class or the audience. This technique will keep a large group attentive, waiting for those all-important moments to shine.

Non-picture book versions of folktales will offer greater depth of content, but may also contain longer sections of narration that must be removed, shortened, or re-written as dialogue. Minor characters or scenes can be cut and any important information shifted to other characters and scenes. Often two characters can be combined into one. If the vocabulary and syntax are too obscure or "literary," substitute more expressive words or split long sentences into two shorter ones.

My favorite material for Story Theatre is classical mythology. It is also my greatest challenge. Many of the stories are sexist and sexy. For the sake of my younger students, I try to work around those danger zones and still capture the power and humor in the tales. I encourage you to work with this material and all of its provocativeness. Your students will embrace the myths and ask for more.

In addition to these traditional materials for Story Theatre, you can also create scripts from biographies, fiction, textbook curricula, and even current events. A creatively scripted and enthusiastically performed Story Theatre can make even dull material sparkle.

In all of my story scripts, I concentrate on using "real language"—language that sounds oral rather than written. You will notice that I use slang, idioms, improper grammar, sentence fragments, split infinitives, and even dangling participles! I explain to my students that although it may be inappropriate language and style for a business letter or a college application essay, it sounds exactly the way lots of us talk in real life.

Methods for Scripting

Scripting can be done as a solitary activity or a team project. The long-term goals for your Story Theatre program will determine the choice you make. If your goals for your students are in the realm of performance, then you may decide to script the story yourself, sitting at your computer, creatively hammering out the script as efficiently as possible so that the bulk of your group time can be spent on perfecting the presentation. If your goals are focused in the discipline of writing, you may decide to spend a greater percentage of time creating the script in large or small groups. Either way you go, the methods I describe below will get you started. The first two are low-tech methods. The third is high-tech, but simple. You can adapt them in ways that work best for you.

But first, before you begin any scripting work, **TELL** or **READ ALOUD** the story. Even if you are working alone, verbalize the material. Ask yourself: Does this story have a life of its own off the page, or must I breathe life into it? Now you have a hint of the work ahead.

Magic Marker Method

1. Make a photocopy of the story—a copy for each person if working in a group.

2. Decide how many characters and how many narrators you'll need. Short stories may need only one narrator, while longer stories will work best with two or more.

3. Choose a different color marking pen for each character and narrator.

4. Underline or highlight the lines each character or narrator will speak.

5. With a black marker, cross out the tag lines—the ones that tell "who said."

6. Where possible, change explanatory material to stage directions: *(QUEEN puts crown on KING's head)* .

7. Draw a box around any long descriptive passages. In the margin, or on the back of the page, condense and rewrite this material as narrator or character lines. If some of the lines now seem unnecessary to the story, eliminate them.

8. If working in a group, each team member should agree on these decisions and mark their copies simultaneously.

9. If the script is short (one or two pages, as for a fable), the cast can begin rehearsing immediately using these marked scripts.

10. The teacher can demonstrate the steps of this process using an overhead projector or a document camera, while the students mark their individual copies.

Cut and Paste Method

1. Make a photocopy of the story—a copy for each person if working in a group.

2. Determine how many characters and how many narrators will speak.

3. Using scissors, cut the paper text into strips, separating each actor's lines.

4. Cut out and throw away any tag lines or passages that you decide not to use.

5. Arrange the strips in order on a new piece of paper, leaving plenty of space between them.

6. Paste, glue, or tape the strips to the new paper.

7. Write the names of the characters or narrators in front of the strips of dialogue.

8. In the spaces you have left between characters' lines, write stage directions and any new material.

9. Make a photocopy of the finished script—one for each person if working in a group.

Projected Computer Method (effective for a large group)

1. Teacher sits at computer keyboard, facing students. Monitor image is projected on screen behind teacher.

2. Type title, author, and genre of story. Be sure to give credit to the scriptwriters who will be creating this new Story Theatre—*"Scripted by Ms. Johnson's fourth grade class."*

3. Ask the students how many characters the story has and how many narrators they would like to use. Type the names of the cast.

4. Show the students how to set up a two-column "table" on your word processing program. (This is the simplest format I've found for typing scripts.)

5. Ask for suggestions on how Narrator 1 will begin the story—*"Once upon a time…," "Long, long ago…"*

6. Create other lines the narrators will speak to give the background for the story.

7. Decide which character will speak next. What will he say?

8. Continue to give and take ideas as the students brainstorm and the teacher types.

9. Stop and save the document when your instructional period ends.

10. For mental homework, ask the students to think about new dialogue, sound effects, and stage directions they might like to add when you meet again to continue scripting the story.

11. When the script is complete, print a copy for each person in the group. They will glow with pride when they see their own words in hard copy!

After you have guided your students through any of these scripting methods once or twice, many of them will begin to develop scripts at their own initiative in their own time. I have observed kids doing Story Theatre on the playground during recess, in the cafeteria before school, and at slumber parties over the weekend. They read, write, edit, and plan every detail of the show. It doesn't matter to them or to me if the performance is less than perfect. The important thing is that these kids have shared a dramatic literary experience with their peers. They have grown intellectually and artistically from the process. That's all the justification I need.

Pronunciation Guide

For most of the Greek names below, I've included the pronunciation most recognizable to most people, whether it is the ancient or the modern Greek pronunciation. For a few, I've included two options (some are regional variations, some based on language derivations, some said differently for reasons unknown to me). Pick the one you're most comfortable saying.

Adriatic . . . . .ay-dree-AT-ik
Aguecheek . . . . . .AY-gyoo-cheek
Alcmene . . . . .alk-MEE-nee
Aphrodite . . . . . . .aff-ro-DYE-tee
Arachne . . . . .uh-RACK-nee
Ares . . . . .AIR-eez
Artemis . . . . .ARR-tem-iss
Atalanta . . . . .at-uh-LAN-tuh
Athena . . . . .uh-THEE-nuh
Augeas . . . . .aw-GEE-us
Bellerophon . . . . .bell-AIR-uh-fon
bovine . . . . .BOH-vine
Brazos . . . . .BRAZ-us
Cerberus . . . . . . .SURR-burr-us
Cesario . . . . .seh-SAWR-ee-oh
          or seh-SAIR-ee-oh
Chimera . . . . .kye-MIR-uh
          or kye-MEE-ruh
          or kim-EAR-uh
Cucullin . . . . .kuh-HULL-in
Cyclopes . . . . .SYE-kloh-peez
          or sye-KLOP-eez
Demeter . . . . .DEM-uh-tur
          or duh-MEE-tur
Diomedes . . . . . . .dye-oh-MEE-deez
dreidel . . . . .DRAY-dull
equine . . . . .EE-kwine
Eurystheus . . . . . .yoo-RISS-thee-oos
Feste . . . . .FES-tuh
Geryon . . . . .gair-EYE-un
Grania . . . . .GRAN-yuh
          or GRON-yuh
Hades . . . . .HAY-deez
Hephaestus . . . . . .hef-FESS-tus
Hera . . . . .HEAR-uh
          or HEE-ruh

Hercules . . . . .HUR-kyoo-leez
Hesperides . . . . . .hess-PAIR-uh-deez
Hippomenes . . . . .hip-POM-in-eez
Hydra . . . . .HYE-druh
Iasus . . . . .I-uh-sus
Illyria . . . . .ill-EAR-ee-uh
Iobates . . . . .eye-OH-buh-teez
latke . . . . .LOT-kuh
Lycia . . . . .lye-SEE-uh
M'Coul . . . . .muh-COOL
Maestro . . . . .MY-stroh
Malvolio . . . . .mall-VOLE-ee-oh
Megera . . . . MEG-uh-ruh
menorah . . . . . . .muh-NORE-uh
Montegolfo . . . . . .mon-tuh-GOLF-oh
Nemean . . . . .nuh-MEE-un
          or NEE-mee-un
Ogre . . . . .OH-ger
Oonagh . . . . .OO-nuh
Orsino . . . . .or-SEEN-oh
Pegasus . . . . .PEG-uh-sus
Persephone . . . . . .purr-SEF-uh-nee
pomegranate . . . .POM-uh-gran-it
porcine . . . . .PORE-syne
Poseidon . . . . .poh-SYE-dun
Poseidonia . . . . . .poh-sye-DOAN-ee-uh
Satyr . . . . .SAT-ur
          or SAY-tur
serpentine . . . . . .SURR-pun-tyne
          or SURR-pun-teen
shames . . . . .SHAH-muss
Sody Salleratus . . .SO-dee sal-uh-RAY-tus
Tiryns . . . . .TEER-inz
          or TIRE-inz
Viola . . . . .vee-OH-luh
Zeus . . . . .ZOOSE

Resources

Ready-to-Use Scripts

These companies offer collections of scripts. Request their catalogs:

Readers Theatre Script Service
P.O. Box 178333
San Diego, CA 92177

Opportunities for Learning, Inc.
941 Hickory Lane, Dept. XE67
P.O. Box 8103
Mansfield, OH 44901

Contemporary Drama Service
Meriwether Publishing
Box 7710
Colorado Springs, CO 80933

Curriculum Associates
5 Esquire Road
N. Billerica, MA 01862

Libraries Unlimited
Teacher Ideas Press
P.O. Box 6633
Englewood, CO 80155

Take Part Productions, Ltd.
Box 86756
North Vancouver, B.C.,
Canada V7L4L3

Phoenix Learning Resources
"Spotlight on Readers Theatre"
2349 Chaffee Drive
St. Louis, MO 63146

Internet

These websites offer teaching ideas and free scripts:

Aaron Shepard's Readers Theater Page
www.aaronshep.com/rt

Whootie Owl Productions
www.storiestogrowby.com

Books

These books include scripts, techniques, educational theories, and suggestions for more resources:

Albert, Eleanor. *Jewish Story Theater.* Los Angeles, CA: Torah Aura Productions, 1989.

Bauer, Caroline Feller. *Presenting Readers Theater: Plays and Poems to Read Aloud.* Bronx, NY: H.W. Wilson, 1987.

Coger, Leslie Irene, and Melvin R. White. *Readers Theatre Handbook: A Dramatic Approach to Literature,* 3rd ed. Glenview, IL: Scott Foresman, 1982.

Davidson, Josephine. *Teaching and Dramatizing Greek Myths.* Englewood, CO: Libraries Unlimited, 1989.

Dixon, Neill. *Building Connections: Learning with Readers Theatre.* Winnipeg, Manitoba, Canada: Peguis Publishers, 1996.

Latrobe, Kathy. *Readers Theatre for Young Adults: Scripts and Script Development.* Englewood, CO: Libraries Unlimited, 1989.

Laughlin, Mildred. *Readers Theatre for Children: Scripts and Script Development.* Englewood, CO: Libraries Unlimited, 1989.

Shepard, Aaron. *Stories on Stage: Scripts for Reader's Theater.* NY: H.W. Wilson, 1993.

Sloyer, Shirlee. *Readers Theatre: Story Dramatization in the Classroom.* National Council of Teachers of English, 1982.

Walker, Lois. *Readers Theatre Strategies in the Elementary Classroom.* Vancouver, B.C., Canada: Take Part Productions, 1990.

White, Mel. *Mel White's Readers Theatre Anthology.* Colorado Springs, CO: Meriwether Publishing, 1993.

Sources and Variants
of Traditional Stories

Myths

King Midas
McCaughrean, Geraldine. *Greek Myths*. Macmillan/Margaret K. McElderry Books, 1992, 1993.

Gerstein, Mordicai. *Tales of Pan*. Harper & Row, 1986.

Arachne and Athena
Osborne, Mary Pope. *Favorite Greek Myths*. Scholastic, 1989.

Morley, Jacqueline. *Greek Myths*. Peter Bedrick Books, 1997.

Bill Erophon and Peggy Sue
Mayer, Marianna. *Pegasus*. William Morrow, 1998.

Yolen, Jane. *Pegasus: the Flying Horse*. Dutton, 1998.

Atalanta
Climo, Shirley. *Atalanta's Race: A Greek Myth*. Clarion, 1995.

Martin, Claire. *The Race of the Golden Apples*. Dial, 1991.

Demeter and Persephone
McDermott, Gerald. *Daughter of Earth*. Delacorte, 1984.

Waldherr, Kris. *Persephone and the Pomegranate*. Dial, 1993.

The Twelve Labors of Hercules
Evslin, Bernard. *Hercules*. William Morrow, 1984.

Burleigh, Robert. *Hercules*. Raintree/Steck-Vaughn, 1999.

The Contest for Athens
McBride-Smith, Barbara. *Greek Myths Western Style*. August House, 1998.

Hamilton, Edith. *Mythology*. Little, Brown, and Co., 1969.

Folktales

Aaron Kelly is Dead
DeFelice, Cynthia. *The Dancing Skeleton*. Atheneum, 1989.

Schwartz, Alvin. *Scary Stories to Tell in the Dark*. Lippincott, 1981.

Finn M'Coul
DePaola, Tomie. *Fin M'Coul: the Giant of Knockmany Hill*. Holiday, 1981.

Byrd, Robert. *Finn Maccoul and His Fearless Wife: A Giant Tale from Ireland*. Dutton, 1999.

Sody Salleratus
Chase, Richard. *Grandfather Tales*. Houghton Mifflin, 1948, 1976.

Davis, Aubrey. *Sody Salleratus*. Kids Can Press, 1996, 1998.

The Squire's Bride
Gross, Ruth Belov. *The Girl Who Wouldn't Get Married*. Atheneum, 1983.

Carter, Angela, editor. *The Old Wives' Fairy Tale Book*. Pantheon, 1990.

The Wolf and the Seven Kids
Kimmel, Eric. *Nanny Goat and the Seven Little Kids*. Holiday, 1990.

Cole, Joanna, editor. *Best-Loved Folktales of the World*. Doubleday, 1982.

The Miller and His Donkey
Sopko, Eugen. *The Miller, His Son, and Their Donkey*. North South, 1985.

McGovern, Ann. *Aesop's Fables*. Scholastic Paperbacks, 1990.

Henny Penny
Wattenberg, Jane. *Henny Penny*. Scholastic, 1999.

Galdone, Paul. *Henny Penny*. Houghton Mifflin, 1968.

Three Billy Goats Gruff
Stevens, Janet. *The Three Billy Goats Gruff*. Harcourt, 1987.

Galdone, Paul. *Three Billy Goats Gruff*. Houghton Mifflin, 1979.

Cat-Skins
Chase, Richard. "Catskins" in *Grandfather Tales*. Houghton Mifflin, 1948.

Cole, Joanna. "Thousand-Furs" in *Best-Loved Folktales of The World*. Doubleday, 1982.

Fiction

Twelfth Night
Nesbit, E. *The Children's Shakespeare*. Academy Chicago Publishers, 2000.

Williams, Marcia. *Bravo, Mr. William Shakespeare!* Candlewick Press, 2000.